LEARN INTERNET OF THINGS WITH

ESP32 FOR BEGINNERS

HAND GUIDE

Sensor and Network, DHT22, Wifi LAN, Ardiuno
Coding, Thingspeak with IOT Project

By

Aharen-san

TABLE OF CONTENTS

INTRODUCTION AND AGENDA 3

GETTING STARTED WITH ESP32..5

GETTING TO KNOW ABOUT ESP32 BOARD.................................13

GETTING STARTED WITH ESP32 INSIDE ARDUINO 19

SERIAL COMMUNICATION BASICS ON ESP32 23

SERIAL DATA READ USING ESP32..30

DIGITAL OUTPUTS WITH ESP32 34

READ DIGITAL INPUTS ON ESP32..39

PRACTICE TASKS WITH DIGITAL INPUT ON ESP32 44

SWITCHING CIRCUIT - DC LOAD SWITCHING...........................47

RELAY SWITCHING CIRCUIT WITH ESP32 49

READING CAPACITIVE TOUCH INPUTS ON ESP32 52

DHT22 SENSOR INTERFACING WITH ESP32...............................57

ESP32 WEATHER MONITORING OVER WIFI (LAN)......................65

WHAT IS INTERNET OF THINGS..70

IOT PROTOCOLS AND THINGSPEAK 79

SENDING VALUES TO THINGSPEAK FROM ESP32 84

DATA VISUALIZATIONS IN THINGSPEAK 91

WHAT IS MQTT PROTOCOL..93

ADAFRUIT IOT PROJECT - PART 2...97

ADAFRUIT IOT PROJECT - PART 3...103

ADAFRUIT IOT PROJECT - PART 4...108

INTRODUCTION AND AGENDA

Let's get started with understanding ESP 32 and 80. This is kind of an official introduction to the project. And in this project we're going to talk about the agenda for this project, what all we are going to do in the schools.

ESP32 and
IoT

Introduction

And we'll get started with starting the as we told you to write to you. So let's get started. Now, this is the project agenda. This is what we are going to do throughout this project. And this is a very rough idea about the project. C One of the benefit of being a developer myself is that I do get to have a number of different problem statements almost every single day. And when I'm creating a project, it's usually a job of 2 to 3 months at minimum. And whenever a new problem statements do come to me, I do include them into the schools as well. So I'll be I'll keep adding all the different problem statements that may come to me during the project of this creation. And then those points will also be there. But roughly what we are going to study or what we are going to cover is what is basically easy to do and why we are going to use it. Then we'll try to understand what are the different boards available for use with 32 and which one we can choose among them.

Course Introduction

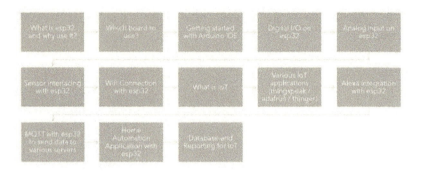

Then we'll get started with the speaker to do programming. In our general idea, we will try to create a simple project or a simple program to blink. It is, you know, kind of Hello World Program for the microcontrollers. Then we'll try to understand the digital inputs and outputs on the SB 32. In the section, there will be a lot of different videos related to facing switches, buzzer and number of different are your devices sort of popular Iot devices which are being used. Then we try to understand the analog inputs on iOS 32. We do some sensor interfacing with analog and digital interfaces. This is the one basics of understanding of microcontrollers. Once we have understood this much thing will move towards the reason why we are using the ISP 32 and there is the Wi-Fi connection on which we'll try to understand the concepts of anxiety and how ESP 32is a very suitable choice for AI. Applications will then try to understand number of different source models for Iot, number of different products, variety, how we can send data to those various platforms and how to shape up our application. We are also going to see the Alexa integration and security protocols, databases and reporting for IATA. So this is going to be a long but really interesting journey for all of us to understand ESP 32and Internet of Things. So let's get started with understanding. It used to be 32 and get started experimenting with electronics hardware. Thank you.

4

GETTING STARTED WITH ESP32

It started with understanding what exactly is ESP 32and why we are going to use one to create applications. Well, the common convention will always see that use. The 32 is a microcontroller, but you should always remember that it's much more than just a microcontroller. In fact, it's a complete system on CHIP or S or C as we developers use to college. Now, why this insourcing? Why not the usual already nodes or extreme 32 of those kind of controllers? There is a reason for it.

What is ESP32?

- Microcontroller?
- SoC System on Chip
- Far complex than general purpose microcontroller
- Meant for IoT Applications
- Developed by expressif systems

The system on CHIP needs an integrated package of a microcontroller, a very big amount of flash memory and coupled with Bluetooth and Wi-Fi. And I built on the same chip with an engine. Now, because of that, what happens is ESP 32becomes a very ideal choice whenever you want to create any connected applications or connected system project for the exec, any kind of applications created, particularly for Iot applications. If you want to have a look at the features of SB 32, I'm not particularly giving it away here because it's much better to see it onto the official website itself.

So I'm going to open the official website that is expressive. The developer of ESP 32CHIP and on the same website will try to see what are the different features available into it. What microcontroller is there? Is it ARM or is it something else then? How many pins are there and what exactly it is better to do? The purpose of this session is to understand what is the SB 32. We are not going to look into the modules, but just the USP 32 I see itself.

So this is the page of SB 32, the official website of expressive systems, and this is the language of ESP 32CHIP. Now, what exactly is this better to do and how expensive creates them? You have to understand this thing first before we try to use it. So SB 32, as we were saying, primarily is an associate order system on CHIP, but expressive also sales. The modules created at launch is better to do, which makes it easier to use them. Now you can see you can either have ESP 32modules or you can have your SU 32 decades documents. Everything is original here. Now, if I go to USP the 32 modules, then I will come to a different page and here you will see what are the different ESP 32modules which are available. The most popular one which we use we are going to use in this project. Also, it's called This is better to do drumset or w r w m Sivits. Now there is a document for this from CID. It's I don't want you to download it. I don't want you to have it. We are just going to discuss it over here because we don't want to go into the exact technical details of the module itself. So I have this module in front of me. Let me finish. This is the module that I should use with 32 from 32 or 32. So what we are interested in is the primary features of this module, how it looks like.

So the module looks like this. As you can see, this is not just the system on chip, but it's a complete module which consists of the antenna as well. So it is built around the ESP 32series of SLC, which is having an extensive dual core 32 bit microprocessor that a number of different flash chip available or flash options available. Primarily the one we use is either A10 B flash or 16 MP flash, which is quite good. Then this module is also having 26 GPUs, all general purpose input output pins. Let's go into the details of this chip and its features so you can see that a number of different peripheral support for design for this module, you can interface SD card and SPI, there is UART, then there is a still eye to see BW motor problem. Then I in front edge but it's counter means timer counters use then the input pin Sophia's filter to do so having capacitive touch inputs we have we do see DSC as well as this additional protocol to WPI. Overall, it's a complete package where you can utilize or connect most of the current and latest embedded interfaces. If you look into the if you look into the Bluetooth side or wireless side of it, so it has got 2. 4 gigahertz Wi-Fi and Bluetooth center frequencies, 241222484 megahertz DVI phase it 02. 11 big end, which is supposedly the latest one. Supports 150 Mbps of data transfer, and we have both Bluetooth version 4. 2 as well as Beat. And the applications are literally limitless with this particular chip. And most important reason why this is so popular around the world is definitely because of the cost. It's a combined package. You don't need a microcontroller and a wireless device to be interfaced with each other and then start building your application here. You can create your application directly from this module. Now, as you can see closely, this is just a photograph for representation. But if you look at it closely, you can see it's a module. Okay. So it's an assembly of surface mounting type module? I don't think so. You can directly use a module that unless you are very good at solving and all the things. So what do we need? Whenever something like this is there, what we need something extra. Just a module will not do for us. So what I will need or what we believe is let's say this is split into two module, then it will need look many different things along with it. So you're going to required a USB interface to download the code. Then you are going to required power supply for this board. Then you are going to require some peripherals. With this fold. Now, what people or manufacturers across the world are doing is they are taking this institute model and then creating a model of their own. So the heart is the hospital to the room. I'll show it to you on hardware. Don't get confused. And then something like this, it's created around it. Like I said, this is called s e s p 32 node MCU. Now, similar to that, I'm just giving you an example of node MCU. But similar to that, there are a number of different modules built around E. S We 32. And if you open any, any electronic stores, for example, in India, let me open Robonaut in, which is one of the most popular stores. So if I open that and for that matter, any such online store and if you search for SB 32, you will be overwhelmed with a lot of different options. And that happens with everyone with starting to experiment with this series of devices. So I just search for is the 32. And if you look at the results, there are lots of them. So nano use with 32 years for 32 audio is for 32 can 18 node MCU yes v 32 OLED module dpkg you see.

And you know, what happens is all of this will get very soon. Very quickly, confusing to you? I'm not saying you cannot use any of them once you understand, once you learn how to use this better to do, you can choose any one of these modules and start creating your project. Even the direct models are also available, as you can see here. But to get to that stage, we need to set a common ground. And for the sake of training project, I have to choose the kind of module which is available here in India, as well as my friends who are taking this project in South Africa or China or in America, in European regions, everywhere. I need a kind of module which should be required or which should be available almost everywhere around the world. Only then we can set a common ground, because previously it has happened with me the same kind of node MCU, which is available over here, maybe available in a different package somewhere else, although they are cheaper. But the the standardization is not there. And that's what makes it difficult to use a board for a project. We need something standard so that whatever we teach here should be easily replicable at your age. And to do that, what we do is we use this approach whose are 32 brought it. We just go to it and just Google it in the fruit. So 32 because I want to show you the official page on Aeroflot website. Now, also 32 is an E ESP 32board created by end of route.

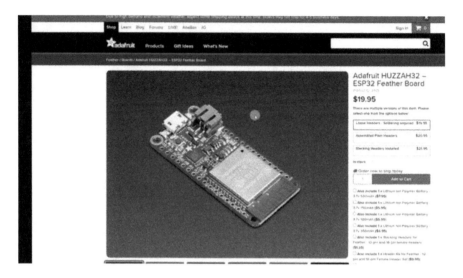

Now in the throat, I guess we all know about it. If you don't know about it means the early end of the simply getting started within. But Systems and effort is a New York based company which creates a lot of different hardware's a lot of different tutorials as well as the cell number of different devices tubes development board the other kids now is maturity is something which is created by end of the call it is better to do Thunderbird now we are going to use this throughout our project. What is the reason for it? The reason is very simple. The same board is available almost across the globe. Anywhere you go you can get to support and if you can't get this, what you can directly order it from it of it. I don't want to go into the complexities of some of your design. These boards, which may be available today, may not be available tomorrow and can still get stuck. No, we want something standard and that's the reason we are going to choose this particular module. The features are listed here itself. If I zoom in the page, which it has got a 240 megahertz dual core microcontrollers integrated for 120 GB of RAM, which is huge for microcontrollers for me. Flash integrated Wi-Fi dual Bluetooth onboard anti now low noise amplifier is in so we'll see why it is used ten capacitive touch interfaces. This is a 32 kilohertz oscillator for RTC. There are three watts, three SBI to A to C 12. It is inputs to two is and to this. Of project, these are all on paper specifications. When you are using the wi fi on DSP 32 chip, you may not be able to we may not be able to use all the features binding we are going to use. E we told you to choose our model by end approach. I have a board with me. Let me show that to you. If you can see this is the is better to do with the module that I have. So it's not going to get focused of support. That's what I am doing and remove that module and just shoot from you will lose up to two further. Okay. So this is the same one that we're going to use here, which you can see in the beach over here. Look at it. This is the back side. This is the backside of my boat. So there should not be any kind of confusion whenever we are experimenting on your splitter.

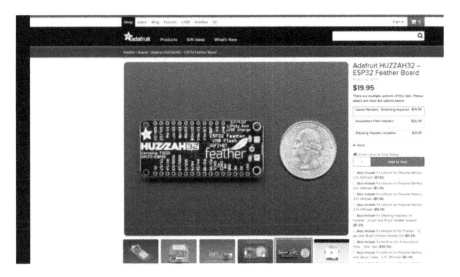

However, if you are confident enough, then you can apply the same learning to any of the other custom boards. Also, it is my recommendation to use this board because my experiment will be done on this page. I hope things are clear for you. So wherever you are, just search for your speed. 32. Who is 32? In your country you will find this center near you and grab a couple of boards. Why? I see a couple of boards because if you are just getting started, most probably you will make mistakes. And when you make mistakes, you immediately find the board or damage on the board. So it's always good to have one more extra at your hands. It never it is never harmful. And in my experience, you will immediately get started with your first board, probably do something, install in your home or sell it as a project. And you will want the another board for sure. You. Watching this video and the next video will get started with experimenting with a spectator to support. Thank you.

GETTING TO KNOW ABOUT ESP32 BOARD

Let's get started with understanding a bit deeper about the aid approach with the 32 or 32 modules that we have selected and we are going to use throughout this project.

ESP32 Chip and Modules

• Various modules makes it easier to use esp32 chip

As I've explained to you before, also the module makes it easier to use the actual USP 32 chip. So this gives you access to power supply, USB interface. The number of ports are very nicely laid out outside. You can see in my board these are the number of pins which are available over here and you will have easy access to them. That's why we use the module and we are going to use this in a module. As we have discussed this already, there are lots of different models available which may cause a lot of confusion. So we prefer to use SB 32. So these are the pictures of the front and back side of this module. When the pins like this are not soldered.

ESP32 Huzzah

Okay, you need to sort of dispense by yourself so that you can inserted into a breadboard for experimenting. Now, let's see what exactly what are the things which are available on the ease with which it could support? Let's try to understand the hardware perspective. Very clear. I want you to focus and understand the session very well, because it may happen that throughout your programming you may be trying to use some particular pin and switch. It is not behaving as it should according to a code. The reason being some of the pins are not useable when you are using file. So just get a clarity about this thing. The entire clarity about the board, although what we can observe here is this is the better connector used with introducer also comes with an onboard battery charger. You may find it a little bit expensive, but considering the utility, it's great. You can directly connect any lithium ion battery, which is 3. 7 volt treated directly to it. And it can start using or you can start using it as before to hit the connector USB cable to this beam and the battery will also get charged. So this is the biggest advantage of having the use with the support. Apart from that, we can notice the USB port interface here. Then there are two tiny bits which you can see over here. This is a reset push button. Then there are some ices over here and this is the exact one. If you turn over your board, then you can also see, because it's an eight effort board there, it's absolutely one of the biggest name in the creation of embedded hardware. Everything is very nicely laid out and written over here. Even the alternate functions. So this experience I do see the CLP as well as the number 22. This is a step in as well as the number 23. So a very detailed care has been taken by the float while creating the sports so as to make our life easier. Let's get started. Now these are the power points on the ECB 32 board. So whenever you have the board in your hand, you have to hold it with the antenna on the right hand side. If I turn it over, you will see it in live concert. But when I observe it like this, from my point of view, it is on the right hand side. So then I'm looking at it like here the pins. Exactly. Besides, the battery connector are back in. And you ask me, these are some of the power pins which are used to power up the is the 32 and on the bottom you can see three volt and ground pin.

Pinout of Adafruit Huzzah32 → Power Pins

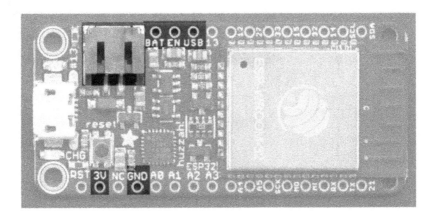

Now, when you're using ausb-c connector, you don't need to worry about any of those things. There is a power supply on it which generates the 3. 3 balls and it is given at this point, if you are not using battery, then you don't need to worry about distance either. We'll discuss that later on when we try to use battery. So just ignore these three pins and instruments whenever you're trying to interface anything with your speed, touch and ignore them positively. Because if you connect something different over here, you may end up frying your chip and you will not even understand it. So just ignore the spins for sure. Next you can see the usable, simple general purpose eye opens on Twitter. What do you see on this slide? What do you see on the current slide? It's all the pins which are directly usable without worrying about anything being number 13, pin number 12, 27, 33, 15, 32 and 14, and then a078283, even a five. So you can use these pins for sure without worrying. We'll discuss about those analog input pins later on. So these are the digital outputs and then these are the analog inputs. Apart from that, we have a secure ACL here and the exotics here will discuss about them. So 20 185848278380 1312 2733 1532 four. These are the pins. Now, why I was a little bit slow down in telling you about analog pins. The reason is here. Is it open is an analog input bin and also an analog output that is called DC two. If you turn it over. That is mentioned there. Yeah, it is mentioned clearly the AC one, the AC two. And like that. Look at here. So this is the DSC to the AC one, things like that. So is it is that. It can also be used as GPIO, and when you use it as a GPIO, you need to refer to it as spin number 26 about PIN number even A1. Again, it is analog input and output, which is DSC one. If you want to use it as a general purpose input output pin, you can use it as pin number 25. Now PIN number A2 A3 if these are purely analog input, pin or general purpose input.

Bottom Row

- **RST , 3v, GND**
- **A0** - this is an analog input A0 and also an analog output DAC2. It can also be used as a GPIO #26. It uses ADC #2
- **A1** - this is an analog input A1 and also an analog output DAC1. It can also be used as a GPIO #25. It uses ADC #2
- **A2** - this is an analog input A2 and also GPI #34. Note it is *not* an output-capable pin! It uses ADC #1
- **A3** - this is an analog input A3 and also GPI #39. Note it is *not* an output-capable pin! It uses ADC #1
- **A4** - this is an analog input A4 and also GPI #36. Note it is *not* an output-capable pin! It uses ADC #1
- **A5** - this is an analog input A5 and also GPIO #4. It uses ADC #2
- **SCK, MO, MI** – SPI Pins
- **RX, Tx** – Uart Pins
- **21** - General purpose IO pin #21

So this is an analog input and also GPI. There is no output facility on PIN number eight to A3. And if that's the reason why I was telling you this is very important, please pay close attention. Then PIN number A5. This is an analog input pin and also GPIO four. So if I was analog input and GPIO for a two, three, four are analog and digital input only is true even are analog input and output, digital input and digital output prints. So this is all dispenser structure and then there are pins over here which are addicts and tags and pin number 21 is a general purpose input output pin.

Top Row

13 - This is GPIO #13 and also an analog input A12 on ADC #2. It's also connected to the red LED next to the USB port

12 - This is GPIO #12 and also an analog input A11 on ADC #2. This pin has a pull-down resistor built into it, we recommend using it as an output only, or making sure that the pull-down is not affected during boot.

27 - This is GPIO #27 and also an analog input A10 on ADC #2

33 - This is GPIO #33 and also an analog input A9 on ADC #1. It can also be used to connect a 32 KHz crystal.

15 - This is GPIO #15 and also an analog input A8 on ADC #2

32 - This is GPIO #32 and also an analog input A7 on ADC #1. It can also be used to connect a 32 KHz crystal.

14 - This is GPIO #14 and also an analog input A6 on ADC #2

SCL, SDA – I2C Pins

Now, the important thing about the analog twins, that's really, you know, one of the one of the very important thing is when you're using wi fi, when you're using a device, which we are anyways definitely going to use, then you can only read the analog inputs on it to pin because all other pins are shared with my family. Just understand that the Ethiopian can only be used as analogue inputs. Of course, not even digital output when you're using the. And my five facility that is provided by this chip. Now, apart from this fence, there is a circuit in my which is over here. You can see a circuit and a mine. This is these are the pins for a second speed. Protocol generally requires four miles. The fourth one, it sits on a chip select. You can use any other peanuts, Chip. Sell it for your spi peripheral. Then there is the exotics, which are the on chip. You want pins pin number 21 a general purpose digital input output. Then on the top side, you can see from PIN number 13. This is also an analog input it well there's also connected to the red LCD next to the device reports. These things are very important. When we are starting to use a microcontroller or when we are starting to use these people, we have to understand which includes two entity, which one goes to analog, which then goes to digital and with ADA Fruit also 32. All those things are very properly little. Then the pain we had besides it has been number 12. It can be used also as an analog input, calling it a 11. This bin has a pulled out adjustability which we recommend using it only at output only or making sure that the pull down is not affected during boot. So let's try to understand that PIN number 12 has to be used only for output purpose. PIN number 27 is also an analog input. PIN 18 on it is to do as the list should be. IO 33 is GPIO 33 also an analog input pin in nine? Now pin number 15 is GPIO 15 and analog input pin it 32 is GPIO 32. Also an analog input pin called a seven. Now this still pins can also be used to connect a 32 kilohertz crystal for on chip artist. In that case, if you are using it, then you will not be able to use this princess GPIO. And lastly, PIN number 14 is there which is also an analog input pin is six, then a cell is there are idle spins only and it is recommended that you do not try to use them as a digital input output. But all in all, you have to understand one thing, that when you are using the ABC a sort of ribbon, you are using device five facility, you can only use analog pin to. Now, this is a very nice representation of the entire board. What each person does, what is the function of your screen? So you can see GPIO 21 and 17 and 16 are just primarily that it so 17 takes. 16 exotics, you can use them.

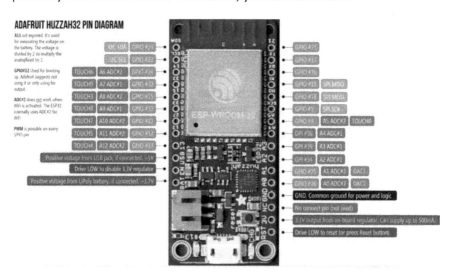

Then the SBI pins is secure. It can also be used through programming as GPIO calling it GPIO 1918 N5. If I pin here what you see is a file and GPO for if you want to use it and this is also touch input. So this is very important and the standard water instrumentation, this will be the main central point of reference point for us when we do experimenting, when we when we create this kind of things in our laps or when we are working on this kind of things in our lab. What we usually do is we take a printout of this particular screen, take a printout of this particular thing because we need it. We are going to need it throughout our experimentation. Where do we connect? What we are to teach and where do these where to do that and all this sort of things? I guess this is pretty much clear to you and enough for you to grasp. This image will also be provided.

GETTING STARTED WITH ESP32 INSIDE ARDUINO

Hi. Let's get started with actually downloading some sample programs into this fruit south32 board. Now, in order to do that, what we need to do is we need to install the Arduino in the computer andwe need to add this board in the board manager of Arduino. I'm considering you have not done anything before. If you have done something on already know much better, it will give a good heads up. But even if you have not done anything, no matter, we'll just do it. Everything right here from scratch. So just let me give you what we want to do. We want to install Arduino in our system, and then we have to add this link into the preferences ofArduino, which will be able to download the inspector to the board. So let's get started. I'll first go to Arduino dot CC and we'll try to download the Arduino software if you have it already. No need to do it again. I just got to software. And I will download the latest Arduino IP. So Windows seven seven and newer best ways to download and install. If you want to donate something just to me, do it annually. So I'll just to download. And now the Arduino software package will get downloaded on your system. Was there already?No installer is downloaded on your computer. All you have to do is just double click the installer file and let your dino get installed. Also remember when they already it's being installed, make sure to click yes to all the driver installationthat it will ask you for. Just start the installation. And I will say yes to any drivers it asks me to install. Just too. I agree. Next, keep the default location. XT and let it get completed. It shouldn't take more than 2 minutes depending upon your computer, but even on much simpler systems,much tinier systems also it doesn't take much time. Alternatively, you can also use alternate clouds, but we prefer having the programs offline on ourcomputer. So even if you don't have access to Internet, which doesn't happen nowadays, but even if you don'thave the Internet access, you would be able to use the programs that you have. It happens sometimes the nature connections get large that it's a problem, and Internet may take an hour for it to restore. And meanwhile, you want to work on something important. So best way is to have everything offline. But conventional thinking. But yes, it is. So already the installation is completed. It has not asked me to install any drivers because in my computer all the drivers are already there. But it will definitely ask you if you are doing the installation for the first. Now let's open the original. And next step is if I go to this presentation, you can see. The next step is to add below link to the preferences of Arduino. We'll see what is preferences. But first, I'll copy this link completely. And now insert or, you know, go to file. But Francis. Here you can see additional border manager orders can be. Installed here. So whatever was there previously? I do not know if it is a blank installation. There would be nothing I have just reinstalled by uninstalling. Therefore I can see some previous stuff. So I have completed this link here and pasted it the same one from the presentation. So all you need to do is just do this file. Click. Okay. Now. What tools? And board manager. And then you will be able to search for ESB to. Now, you see, it's better to do this already installed on my computers. As I told you, I removed the Dino and reinstalled it. Therefore, the board definitions and everything remains the same over here. Still, what I'll do is I'll try to install the latest one, which is 2. 0. 1. Remember installing XP 32, Bolt is installing a completely new French compiler altogether for use by32. So it may take some time. As you can see here it is 148. 976 KB It means one almost 149 maybe you can see, which is not a very small slice to download. Therefore just wait for it to be completed and then will continue with the experiment. Another download has been completed. It will take its own time depending upon your Internet speed as well as the speed of your computer. Download and then install the ISP through the works. Meanwhile, what you can do is if Arduino it's connected to your computer. So this is micro USB cable I'm having, which is required for the ISP 32 support to work. So I'll just connect the cable over here. And if I have a driver installed, then you will hear a beep. Which you can do is go to device manager on your computer. And see if you can see a complete coming up. Now see silicon labs sleep 210 Excuse me to divide bridge. This one is a complete funnel rDNA. Now what I'll do is or is better to do with Zavod. Not always remove my original. You can see that one world has vanished. So whenever you connect it, you'll get to see the complete number. If it is not coming up, it means you need to install drivers for this. You split 32 or 32, but most of the times the drivers are already installed. But if they are not, then you can simply search for speed. 210. To use what we what bridge drivers, it is very straightforward and simple to find and you can install it. Let's see. The Arduino board installation is completed. Now, what I'll do is I'll try to use or I'll try to select. The article is better to do bold or huzzah authority to board from the board manager and I will try to download a blink program. Let's see. So in your original installation, by default, if you go to tools and if you go to bold, you will for sure see Arduino as your default board selected for the fresh installation. But when I go to this option here, I can see I have already know if you are boards and then there is32 Arduino boards. Now what we want to do is we want to go to ESP 32bolts audience for 32 original boards. And we want to find out this particular board here. Our depth route is to do feather in the fruit is better to do feather. I have selected the ADA Proteus with 32 Federal Board on every Arduino board. You know that there is a built in LCD. Sometimes it is connected to pin number 13 on it or do not know in case of board like was that 32. You can see it here, the onboard LCD. It's connected at Richmond. Let's try to find out over here. So I guess it's some had discussed it. So on this Saturday to further about the LRT, there is an on board you can see over here, which isa red colored one, a followed on. It's connected to pin number 13. So also it is it and touch input. Let's try to read the program footage. So this is a convention meeting or do you know that the building is referred as the building? Whatever is aboard it will try to get rich, but we'll just try to make it 13. If you are not aware of the typical Latino programming set up, then and every original program consists of two primary things. So what is called a void setup and another one is called void loop. What a setup. It's something that executes only once and void loop. It's something that includes forever. So whatever you write, don't end. World Loop is your main program that you need to be looped in continuously forever. Let's say it's the temperature logger on the cloud. So you want to read temperature? Send it over to cloud. Let's say wait for 5 seconds against the temperature. Send it over to cloud for 5 seconds. So this should come in your loop. But in order to use the temperature sensor, in order to connect to the network, you need to do some initialization that you will do in void setup. If you are completely unaware of the coding structure of Arduino, don't worry. As we go on, we will try to understand things easily. So first thing we need is our first thing we write is in setup we write bin more 13 comma output and then we wrote in our loop digital right 13 comma high digital right 13 comma low. Now that's a very simple blank program that I'm going to do and I will save it as let's say I'll just create a folder on my desktop, I'll call it is with 32 codes. I'll just call it Blink. I have saved this. What I'll do is just to make things simpler. Keep the delay of 2 seconds. Now we're all set. The last 432 board selected. Then you need to select this comport again. Look at your silicone laps use, but divide bridge, come set content. So select content in the ports. And then you're ready to upload the code. Just click on this button upload and you will see the code will start uploading onto the board. There is a narrative which is fostered when the code has been downloaded. I'll show you that. But first, let's see how the court downloads and how we can see the output on our entity. So you can notice the state associate for now. What it is doing is it is trying to compile the sketch was the sketch compilation is done. It will try to upload that onto the Feather 32 or ESP 32Effort Board. Let's wait for a couple more moments so you can see the progress. But here you can see the progress. Message is here, let it get finished completely and then we'll be able to see. Now see it is uploading, connecting the writing, writing, writing, writing a lot of statistics, leaving hardly sitting. Where is it now? You can see the court is downloaded. Can you notice the only blinking with a delay of 2 seconds? On for 2 seconds. For 2 seconds and for 2 seconds. Offer 2 seconds. Look at it. You. Now, this is the lady that I was talking about, which appears or which blinks when you're trying to download a code. Now, what I'll try to do is I will try to reduce the delay to 500 milliseconds, and I'll try to upload it once again. Now you'll see. Well, applauding again, this lady will be blinking continuously or very fast. Now it is compiling the sketch for now. This is the foster. Mostly this is uploading. The uploading process had started. It's finished. And now you can see the blinking faster. So this is the first and most important thing that you will do whenever you get a new Arduino board. So I hope this is clear to you how to do this processes. The presentation is given to you in which you can copy the link from. And just get started with your 32 board and then continue further understanding the different interests.

SERIAL COMMUNICATION BASICS ON ESP32

Hi. In this edition, we'll try to understand how to perform the communication between ESP 32and a computer. Now, definitely there would be a question why we want to work with Syrian communication first. And I do experiment a lot with all the projects that I create. And I have found that working with Syrian communication first clarifies a lot of different things and it gives you an easy and quick output device to start working. Besides, the libraries and vaults are simple to use, and therefore I think starting with Syrian communication would be a good point for you into the world of yes, we have to do embedded systems and Iot, so let's get started. First of all, let me get back to the basics of serial communication. So in order to understand that, what I'll do is I'll try to open my white book because it gives me quite a good. Well, space to explain things. Okay. So let's get started. When was this initial communication? What we want or what we mean needs? It's whatever microcontroller you have. In this case, we have 32. But it doesn't matter which one it is. So whatever microcontroller you have has to communicate with computers. And why do we need to do that? Because serial communication is the simplest way to communicate between devices of Syrian interfaces like computers, but not limited to only computer. In the same way, you will be interfacing to a Bluetooth module. Sometimes you also interface with other interface ships and like many different peripherals like ships, GSM. RFID reader and so on. Now with respect to computer, there is one issue computer doesn't have. I mean, at least the laptops doesn't have of making cereal. So what we do is we use a USB to cereal interface. And the beauty with every Arduino compatible board, including the ES with 32, is it comes with an onboard USB interface. So an alias with 30 to work if you're looking to do schematic, I have some very indisposed version here because if you look at here this I see over here speed 102 or 2104 is useful to you on bridge.

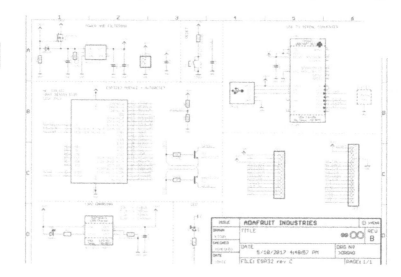

So the microcontroller will communicate with this ESI using two lines or less. SD And you can see those two landscapes as well as you. We send the data using the DMZ line, using asynchronous communication, and we assume they talk to the Annex two line on the controller. This I see acts as a bridge to interface with the USB port of your laptop or your computer. Would you ever use it? So things become simpler in this city when you try to interface with this. However, there is one thing to understand, and that is this is all synchronous communication. Primarily this it's asynchronous means launch. In asynchronous communication that is not block share between E ESP 32and the computers. On any communicating device. So the clock is not shared. And because of that, we don't have a way to synchronize between the bits which are being sent. What I meant to say is if I'm sending something like this, then. Is this single one on? This is 1101 or this is 111001. We don't have any means to identify that. What is exactly one? What is the duration of one? What is the duration of zero? We don't know that we cannot synchronize because the clock is not synchronized. And because of that, what we do in asynchronous it in communication, it's synchronized with this speech. A very simple example. It's I'm pretty sure you come across people from lot of different geographical backgrounds, a lot of different places. And you may have observed that some of them have a tendency to speak faster, probably, or speak slower. Now, when you work together, when you become friends for the first time, would you say to each other is you talk to him or her? That means go a bit slower. He or she talks to you that is going faster and adjust your communication speeds in the exact same manner. What we do is we match the speed at both devices. This speed is called let's mix for a second. Which.Also called outrage. Now, there's a lot second thought about it. There are some standard definitions by IPC which are used. But the most popular one, it's mentioned zero zero which is being used and top of the land. It is 115200. So you can see that the communication is happening at one of the explosive objects most commonly. However, it is not limited to you can use any if you want. So what we have to do is we have to set the scene which split second voltage at the transmitting or one device and the same one at the other device so that internal clocks are synchronized with each other and therefore whatever data is in sent, it will be properly identified. So it may very well be the case that this is 111110000. This is one one. Doesn't matter. Whatever is the detail sending, it will probably be synched between the two devices if the mode matched. So this is what we're going to do and we can perform two way communication in it. There are a lot of different things like Blix will replace, but I will not go into those intricacies because those are not important to you. What we can do, however, here, is understand one thing that we have two separate lines density and objects so we can transmit and see, but not at the same time. Usually it is half the communication. And you can also do it at the same time, also in some cases.

Now that we have got some understanding of the serial communication, let's see what are the different library functions available in order to perform the system communication? So what I've done is I have listed some of the most widely used or you can see most used function here. However, the library's quite comprehensive. I'll also show you that where you can see for the references and how to get a better understanding of all of the functions. But to start with, these are some of the functions that we are going to require that we're going to need. So Serial or begin is a function which we will be using to start the communication. We need to specify objects on which you. Then civil rights is a function which is used to send a single byte on a serial device from microcontroller from USP 32 to the other device. Cylinder print function is a very nice function that you can bypass either a single byte, autocomplete, extreme, or even a variable. It will convert whatever you post which to ASCII and it will be sent to the other device. Similarly dated serial print Ellen which also prints a new line along with this asking that your percentage. Cylinder available is used to check if there is some data coming on the serial code for reception and still not read is used to read the data. Now without spending much time over here. Let's try to understand the program in action. So I just discard this and I'll open a blank. Or you know what, skip and start writing a program. Now lets start typing some code. As I said, the very first thing we need to do is Syrian docs begin. So Serial is the class name that we use and begin is the function. And here you need to specify about, for example, specifying 9600. It's a very common practice to give a small deal to get the serial module initialized. Well, so we put in, you know, ten milliseconds, 100 milliseconds. And in one of the what I like to do is I try to bring something on the serial. So serial French alarm, which will also present a new line. Welcome to ECP 22. The serial communication. And let's put a delay of, let's say, 2 seconds. So delay function here will give you the delay of a specified number of milliseconds. Let's try to save this score and see which in the same location so that you can have the access afterwards. And I will call it serial. Yes. Okay. Now, let's try to upload the score into the controller. So what tools? Select Board. We have selected it right then Select Board. We have selected it based upon our configuration and then upload the program compiles first. It is for data due to which compiler which is we have already installed on the audience. It usually takes some time to install, make sure that the board it's connected to a computer. I'm using a desktop system here. I do prefer it because things remain the same in the same place. So whichever you use it, just make sure the board is connected and now you can see the program is downloaded. Now we want to see this output. Where is it and where is it printing this? Welcome to yes. We try to do serial communication and all. So in order to see that we need a different software called this terminal, a terminal can open your serial ports, whether they are physical serial port like those are in desktop or later.

Those are the US which are serial virtual homeworks which are provided by the boards like he is talking now. In order to do that, we have to use a different software but already provides a built in utility. It's called a serial monitor. If you can see it in tools, you can see serial monitor. You will find the same thing here. Also on the top right corner, look, two on the top, right corner. So if I click on this button, it will open the serial monitored. If you can see the serial monitor has opened and the data it's coming from microcontroller this you can see here the state is already selected as sensitive. But if I do choose something else, see what happens. So the data still coming, as you can see, but the computer is not able to interpret it properly. So some garbage values are shown. If I choose a lower power, if I choose a higher about which.Something. Same is going to happen if we don't understand what we're actually getting and losing. That's gombrich because the interpretation is getting it all. So in order to correctly interpret it unique, you use the same model which has been used in your program. When I see 9600, then you will see the text that is coming. Starts making sense. So this is the simplest way to send data to computers. Let's try to see something more. Let's say we have a variable. I declare a global variable for this purpose and I is equal to the zero. And let's say we want to print this variable on the input as well. So now what I do is welcome to serial communication. I equal. Instead of print. Ellen What I know is a blueprint only because it will then not print a new line. And I can print either just besides this line and then print it. You'll get it. And then sell the print and I. And then I'll simply do what? Hopelessness. So whenever the I it sense to see the import, it will be incremented by one. So I'll do control you, which is a shortcut for uploading the code on to the board. And you can see the compiling had started. If we could combine completely and then it will be downloaded onto the board.Uploaded to sea.Technically an already notorious Nazi. It's connecting the 1919, 19, writing, ranting. And so let's open serial port. Lucy Read started with one because the zero was already printed. In that case, what I do here is I just reset my board once. You see. Welcome to serial communication is equal to zero. Then one, then two, then three.Four.And so on and on. So this is how you can print of Feinerman onto the Syrian communication channel. I'll send a variable to Syria communication channel. One thing is interesting. The zero is actually a decimal zero. It's not ASCII. The Cyrillic print alone will convert it to s. However, if I don't see it elegant right then it will indirectness in zero as it is to the computer. And if I open a browser and if I look to ask it.Shocked. Then you will see in this ASCII chart Z2 is let's see what did zero so zero which startled me. Well. We see some of image.

Decimal - Binary - Octal - Hex – ASCII
Conversion Chart

So zero is actually null. One is associated with something. Three, It's something and a lot of characters. After 48, it starts with one and they will get to zero and then onwards. So let's try it first. Let's see what happens when I write the zero one and so on, and then we'll try to see the other things. Cause I don't want to confuse you, but I do want to understand the difference between right and print and tell it. There's a reason why I'm giving you this example. One problem is there because it looks like it will not go into new line. What will do it? Settle down and just put in a blank new line for things to get easier because then it will come in the new line. So now it's compiling. Once it's uploaded, I just click to see monitors. Now you can see. So we are not actually sure. Okay. I just opened the board first, so I monitor first. So the photos are downloaded. That is Ed. Let's properly download the code and then only open this little monitor. This volume doesn't happen with the regular art in the works, but he we tend to do something different and it has been made to work with art. So certainly do art. Now the downloading is going on. Then open the cereal box. Nothing. There is a box again. A box again. A box solicited. Zero one, two, three. For.Five. Six with a delay of 2 seconds is coming. The first printable characters will be absurd at 33, which is you can see. Which is the exclamation mark before that. All of the characters are not going it. We cannot wait that long. So let me just start with something. Three settle and let's leave a delay of 1/2 and sort of. To. Let's see what

29

happens after this code is downloaded. Now the uploading had started a lot on the Syrian port and soon as the downloading is uploading us to. Again, you'll see a box, but now you'll see the characters started coming in. So 1331 or maybe even 30, and then 31 and then 33 onwards. You can see the printable characters are coming. If we wait for a bit long, then we'll also start to see 48, 49, 50, 51, 52, 53, four, 55, 56 and so on. So these are the decimals which, when directly given to a device for printing, will be interpreted as the obstacle and the respect to us. The character which is represented by that form will be printed. You will require this a lot in coming times. So just make sure that when you are printing a variable and you know, representing that you'll see the bridge unless there is an explicit needed to your serial or light, don't use that.

SERIAL DATA READ USING ESP32

Now that we have done with serial test, what I'll try to do now is I will try to create a serial lead program. Now let's started with some basics. Let's begin. 9600. We'll just have to meet with Larson because we took time to open the input. So it's better if we have a meatless or Delia. Then what we'll do is we'll try to do this. Now, I want to read it from cereals. So before I directly need a film cereal. But let me tell you how it works. So whenever you send something to the microcontroller, it is stored in a cereal buffer buffer. It's kind of a temporary storage which holds whatever data is coming to the cereal box. Usually the forsythe's depends on on the board you have but a very common factor on a very common name number on the cereal buffer of our DINO. It's 64 bytes or 156. So those are some of the common numbers you can go into the libraries to understand about them. But to get started, we don't need to worry about it. When time comes, I'll tell you about it. So the thing is data to us to send into this buffer and then only you can use cereal dot need in order to see this data. And if you don't have anything to read, then you will probably end up reading blank because there is nothing in the buffer. So therefore, in order to understand if the data is received or not, we need to have a function. The function in Syria is not available. So still not available is the function and it returns the number of bytes from the city. Okay. So if that is the case, then how do you use it? Using is very simple, actually. So if so, a lot of the label is greater than zero. What it means, even if a single character is really then this if condition is strong and will be executed. So if serial dot available is greater than zero. And then what we want to do is we need some variable to store this. So let's say entity is it will do city or not. Okay, so we read it in serial note. We're using serial or data function in table called a and then. Then what? We'll try to bring it back to the computer. Now, you have to understand that when you enter something from the computer, you have always entered ASCII. Even if you have entered zero, it means you're sending 48 and so on. And therefore, if I have to print it back to the computer, I should not use the interpreting function and instead I should see the look like function before I send it to B, C or Lewis I can delete and then I'll know what. Serial dot print e.The same man. And then when I lose it are not Ellen and the blank line. I'm sorry. I misprint here. It looks very much, as I mentioned. So whenever something is received after 3 seconds, the same might be sent back to the beast. Let's see how it works. Let's upload this code for now. And once the uploading is done, we'll try to see how it works. If you want, you can also do some hello welcome or something here which will indicate that the programme had started. The biggest advantage of serial communication, apart from the usage for system communication actually is debugging. It's easy when you go into when you go in to creating advanced, advanced embedded systems. Many times you'll find a move that you don't know.

```
void setup() {
  // put your setup code here, to run once:
  Serial.begin(9600); delay(3000);
}

void loop() {
  // put your main code here, to run repeatedly:
  //Serial.available() it returns the number of bytes ready for reading
  if( Serial.available() > 0) // even if a single char is ready, then this if condition is true and will be executed
  {
    int a = Serial.read();
    delay(3000);
    Serial.write(a);
    Serial.println("");
  }
}
```

A particular piece of code is being executed or you don't know if you have written some commands to learn something from something and you don't know whether it has been received or not. So in those places, you use the serial brain function as a debugging tool. We just think, let's say hello. Okay, I come up to here. I came up to there in your code in multiple places. This will help you a lot. And you'll find that experimentation. So the code is downloaded from the serial monitor and it started to bring something. So let me first view Capital E over here. So I have the capital E and I'll just click on the send button. 1 to 3 seconds. We've got the capital E back. Let me put zero here and cents. One, two, three. And we got zero over here. So this is how you do it from Seattle port and you take it back. If you want to be a bit more experimental with what we do, then you simply do serial or write. It looks like this. Or what'll happen is if you have given zero, one, seven and eight in this country, you have given small C, then you will assume small B and so on. So these are the most common functions, most common ones which are useful serial communication. And. To get started. This is enough. Now let me give. Let's see. Capital B. And then after 3 seconds, one, two, three, after 3 seconds, we supposed to get an E, whatever you pass if I give one. And then after 2 seconds, I'm supposed to get something else. When you give the send button, then what happens is you also send a new line character from computer and therefore addition one to that is also disabled, which is why you're seeing

becomes zero. It means close to computation. Now, when it becomes 3.3, which the LCD turns on. Now, what does that exactly mean? Now, to understand that, let's try to see the schematic of BSP 32. Okay, so here I have the schematic of use with 32. Just try to look at this section over here so we can see there is a resistor and an LCD which are connected to IO 13. IO 13 is the PIN number 13, which we referred to.

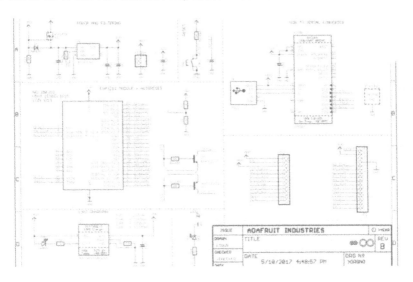

So when we write Digital Note My Heart, what happens is this thing becomes 3.3 world. That is it as a stop. And the control of the reality is going to. This is the reality that we have observed. On to the. Bold. I can also show it to you now. It's working. So this has been number 13 here, which is blinking. It's this one here. Now, what it means is it means if it ever can connect like this on board, then we can also definitely connect multiple such entities apart from the outside of the books, and we can link them. So let's see what I'm talking about. For all this purposes, this what I'm going to do is I'm going to use an online socket to show you this schematics. I will also be including the schematics into the master presentation so that you don't have to worry about a lot of different documentation. So I'll play a few and a schematic there. Everything will be the single presentation final. For now, let's go to the schematic that I have tried to prepare. So this is how you can create a schematic. Now, this is only for connecting for relatives to ISP temperature, but likewise you can connect and then it is on whatever it is you want. Give us an entity must be connected with this. It is registered to the pin of we touch it whenever you go high on that. When we become 3.3, this one kit is still very limited. The current flowing to the entity to 2.3 million peers and you're done all liquids you can connect this one, this one, this one. The control of the ammunition go to ground and all should come to the controller beam. The placement of resistor is your choice. You can keep the first resistor of later of resistor first and later.

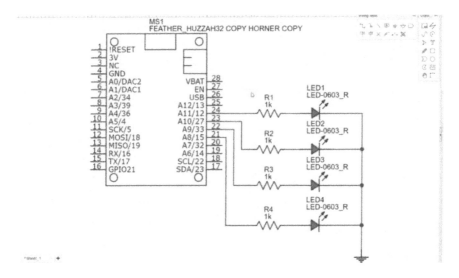

Many of the designers, mostly newcomers, have a confusion that we have to have energy first, and then there is also we have to have the register first and then the end. There is nothing like that. I have just created this to make it simpler. However, just to make the point clear here, there is no difference in connecting it like this and it's the current only flows when you also disclosed. So it doesn't matter whether you connect that it is to before or later. What matters is you must connect the and it's still possible. Now, if you create a socket like this on a blade, but using LSD and resistor, then you will be able to blink for different entities at a time. Also, what kind of footage? See here. Here we have PIN number 12, 27, 33 and 50. I have checked all this can be used as a digital footprint and therefore you can use VIN number 12, 27, 33 and 15 now and you can modify your code accordingly. So let's try to create another program here. I will just try to close this one. Now, instead of referring to them as in numbers, what I'm going to do is I'm going to give them some flexibility, one and two. So that to do that with a simple just note integrity one is equal to. Well. And similarly copy paste it three more times. I use a mechanical keyboard, so I guess that will be a problem for you. You might be getting some ticks, but it will stay the nights when you write the code. 2733. 50. 27. 13. I'm using the 33 and 15. I think that would be. Now if you are using 40 entities at a time or for that matter elderly is at the time, it doesn't matter. All you need to do is you need to do more of each. So more energy output. Now in the similar context we will go on alluded to in addition and you have to make sure to make all of them work as outputting. Without that, you can not generate output on the spins. Now let's assume that I want to make all of those spins higher, enter time and then low after some delay. So what I do is I like digital, right? And even my higher again, I will do a lot of copy wasting and I expect you to do the same. Don't become a typewriter. Be able to grammars. Okay. A very classic cliche line used by software industry, but it is true indeed. So all of them made higher. And now all of them I'll make. No, I don't even like low multiple times and such. And now all I'm going to do is I'm going to download that into your speech review board. All I have to do is all the settings of there already enthusiast, etc. to further contain everything is there to just click on the upload button. Before that, you have to save to score. So they have created a folder for it. Let me call it for idiots. So it's been saved. Now you will notice the yellow will blink very fast after the compilation is done. And then the quarter we were down. Now, as you can see, the program has been uploaded onto the board. And the one which was blinking before the bulletin had stopped. Now did spins. 1227 3315 are now blinking. But no one quibble with it. I will have to create a schematic like this on it. So you need that distance and you did. And it is in order to create this kind of schematic when creating the project. I want things to be simpler for myself and faster so that I can demonstrate to you. That's what I'm going to show you, that I have created a very simple book. Okay, it looks like this. I have created this particularly for one purpose. I will share with you the schematic as well as the layout also so that you can create one for yourself. The benefit of this building is it has got. Let me take the camera out and I will explain it to you better. So as you can see here. It has. What? If it's over here, then I have got four switches. Then I have a really a buzzer that is LCD. That is a real time clock. There is motor driver. There are lots of interesting stuffs over here. So if I use this one, then it will probably make my life. Is it what I'm going to do? I'm going to insert this USP 32 into a breadboard so that I can take wires out of it. And I will make the connections. However, please note that the connections remain exactly like this. As you can see, I'm screwed. Just give me a moment and I'll make the connections. Hi, Nancy. Kinsey. See, I made the connections from this into this and more towards my. An absolute vendetta to do.

All I have done is common. The grounding of our way to the ground of divorce.Divorce, common. And then this four points over here in number 12, 27, 33 and 15 are connected to four different entities. My board might be getting a bit older, so the brightness of it is different. But you can see the difference. You can see the blinking I've used. Now let me try something different. Let me make it 505 hundred as my. Well, let's see if you can notice the change in attitude. The code is being uploaded. Now the campaigning is going on. And it's uploading, though. And the uploading. It's done. Did you notice over here in this window? Sorry. All of them are blinking halo, halo, halo with a delay of 5/2. So 500 milliseconds. So this is just for the understanding of how do we generate output on multiple spins on DSP to do to book and the upcoming sessions. We'll see how we can interface with buzzer relays, switches and like many different things.

READ DIGITAL INPUTS ON ESP32

Hey. Now that we have understood how we can use the switch and pull up our freedom configuration, let's try to connect the switch externally to ESP 32and let's try to see how to use it. So in order to do that, what I'm doing is I am going to connect the two switches like this is with the two to work. If you are using a breadboard, then you can connect the two switches or keys like this as a slim, because I'm using a very simple interface boat which has got some switches on to it. So any delays in them? Nevertheless, this is how the connection should be. One switch, it's connected to PIN number GBI as well. And another one is Digital Yellow 27. Now, the other point of the switch is directly going to them. If we just make some corrections, this. We'll look at. So now this is how my switch connections are connected. Now, you might be wondering why you have not connected any pull ups, because the yes, we are due to boot the white suit with internal pullups, which can be an effort now to enable them to see enough of them. So there is nothing much to explain. The rhetorically jump to the corner. So I have a new sketch artist program taken here. Seemed as a switch test. I have written it. Which test? Nurse stick word setup. And why. Look. And I'll declare the truce, which is like this, in which one is equal to 12 and switch to is equal to 27. As you can see over here.So 12 and 27.Now in setup. What I'll do is I'll just initialize the serial box so that we can send some information on the sit footprint of this, which is first and then the next instructions, important sequence, pin mode, switch one comma input and pin mode, switch to command input. Now to understand one thing very accurately that when you specify input, it means the pins will by default be translated. It means you will have to connect an external pool of water. Don't if you have to use the input like this. Otherwise if you want.Connecting the switch like I'm doing. Then what we can do is instead of writing input, we'll just write

39

down input, underscore, pull up. Now when you write input, underscore, what happens is the internal followups to the switches are enamelled and now in action. And because of this internal collapse, what happens? The different stage which is read all the time, it's high and only when the switch is pressed, then the status of the switch may become low. You release the switch, it again becomes higher. Now let's see how to detect that. And of project, the function is very simple. It's called digital root. Now I will use that in an if conditions. If digital did switch one, it's low. Then I want to do something. What? Let's see. Let's do similar print and then switch on. It's pressed. Let's take some B lesson. Now what it does is, what did we do? It's. It's very simple. Whenever you press the switch, this if condition will execute. And because it executes those said you will see some message on positive that could switch one expressed. Now we do the same thing for switch to no much changes in the program as such. So f digital will switch to is equal to equal to blue. Then let's French switch to its best. That's simplistic.

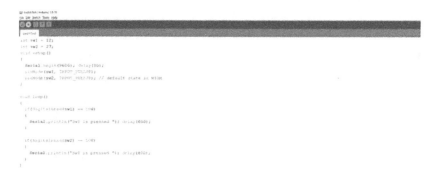

Let's turn to see the output of this school, then upload the program. Now let me clear my desk. I also happen to have a light here, but I have cleared the desk a bit so that I can now show you the camera. Okay, there is an error. I missed semicolon here, so just please bear with my desk. It is usually always messy because a lot of gates and the connecting wires and everything out here. But I guess that should be okay. And you might be able to correlate with me when it comes to your work desk, when you are experimenting on electronic gadgets. The code has been updating, has been Stockton and it's done. So I just opened the serial monitor and what I'll do is I'll just use the camera to show you the actual set that I'm having. Just a moment. So this is the setup I'm having. You can see these are the two switches that I have. I have connected the first one. And the second one to is Vince.Vince, the number 12 and the number 27, which you may not be able to spot that usually in this way. And that's why I have given you a schematic. Now I'm going to press the switch the switch one. Okay. And look at the switch one press as well as on to the sit in moment. So switch when pressed. You can see, as long as I keep it pressed with a delay of 600 milliseconds, the message keeps coming. So which one is blessed? I didn't judge press the switch to. You can see switch to express the messages coming and as long as you keep it pressed, the message will keep coming. You limit the messages gone. Again, let me try and switch one. Now, see, as long as the switch is pressed, the program keeps repeating itself. Now what we can do in order to make this not happen. Okay. What I'll do just now for some time is I'll just put it over here, the camera. Let's say I don't want this to happen. So then I press the switch one. It's continuously coming in and out of it, but it's still continuously coming in. I don't want that to happen. Now, in that case, what you will do. You have to understand that this delay is particularly given for the same reason. The primary reason for giving this delay is it induces a time which is required for a user to press and release the switch or for a single switch press. Now, let us assume that if you have not had time, delay this to moment. Okay. No. I have downloaded the score. Remove the delay. Now, see, when I press the switch, what happens? Even if I press and immediately the message it has been executed. One, two, three, four, five, six, seven, eight times same. We switch two and it is unpredictable. The longer you keep it pressed, the more the data keeps coming. Why? Because the delay of press and release is not induced. So first thing, in order to ensure that it doesn't execute multiple times the added unit. And furthermore, if you don't want a rapid execution to happen at all correctly, what's happening? It is going into the slope of this condition. This particular code, it's executed, then a delay, and then it comes here. It

41

again ticks back to the first condition. If it's straight true, then this is executed. Now I can do something to avoid it being deliberately executed altogether. What I can do is very simple. So just look at it. So while. Digital read. So which one is equal to or equal to low? I will repeat. Vitamins are basically I can put the empty semicolon like this opening and closing it once. I'm just writing a while loop, but I have not written anything in there. The same can also be replicated ads by simply give me a semicolon over here. I'll repeat the same thing. In this case there was switch to is low. I will just wait to see what happens as an output of this scopes. So let me focus back again on this sutures and how the setup, the completion had started. And the program downloading is also starting to stutter. So. The upload procedure is done. I will open the cinema monitor. Okay. Now I want to press the switch and I'm going to hold it. Okay. So this is the switch I'm going to press and I've pressed it. Now see, I have hold the position, but still the court is executed only once. It's not executing again. Same way. If I press it again, then it will be executed once and it is not waiting at the one condition as long as it is law. We don't want to do anything. We just wait here and then it's again, switch to release. Now you see, while releasing sometimes it may come back again because there is a D bounce in the switch press itself. But I hope you got the idea of how these things are managed. If you don't want the even the slightest delay that is happening, then you can add a bounce. Demands delay is a very small, you know, the time required for the contact to be completely made or to be completely open. So basically a switch is nothing but like a contact. So very you make a contact and get it to release it. So has the living also looks like this? It makes like this.

```
int sw1 = 12;
int sw2 = 27;
void setup()
{
  Serial.begin(9600); delay(10);
  pinMode(sw1, INPUT_PULLUP);
  pinMode(sw2, INPUT_PULLUP); // default state is HIGH
}

void loop()
{
  if(digitalRead(sw1) == LOW)
  {
    Serial.println("sw1 is pressed "); delay(600);
    while(digitalRead(sw1) == LOW);
    delay(20);
  }

  if(digitalRead(sw2) == LOW)
  {
    Serial.println("sw2 is pressed "); delay(600);
    while(digitalRead(sw2) == LOW);
    delay(20);
  }
}
```

It releases like this. It makes like this. Delicious like this. And it takes a very short do that. So 20 milliseconds sufficient for the buttons. Now there will not be any repeat execution also because now even after the switch becomes higher, it will wait for 20 milliseconds before executing exiting this condition, which is enough for the demands to execute. These are the core fundamentals of accepting a digital input on any microcontroller overall in your system. So I want you to experiment with everything in detail. Digital. Now, see, I'm going to press the switch. And I'm going to release it now. No matter how you press it and how you release it. You will not see a double exclusion switch to, if you remember, last stance, which was given almost always a double execution that is inherent in the nature of the beast, which is that to is indeed a mechanical conduct. So a mechanical contact will never be made like instantly, never been released instantly. They will always play like this. And therefore we have added this demands to never, ever, ever. You will see that there is any kind of response now. So this is all for now. This is what you can see as the fundamental of accepting that digital inputs on iOS.

PRACTICE TASKS WITH DIGITAL INPUT ON ESP32

Hi. Now that we have seen the sample program with Switch, I have few tasks for you to execute. I'm going to show you one of them. And I would like you to execute some of them, either one of them using your own practice. Actually, there are a number of different tasks, which I would just add. So what I want you to do is create an app. Don't this and switch then a simple entity control using switch the two elements and dosages. Then one switch. It's pressed both on and when. And then switch is both again to erase and to switches. And this time, what I want you to do is I want you to do a little control on individual switches. When one switch is pressed and ready one on, then the other switches pressed and it is one off and. And you do two on. So these are some basic tasks I would like you to do with sutures. Okay. I'll just show you this tool so that you get an idea of how to do that. And then you can continue with the other things. So I've done control using switch. First of all, let us copy this entire code. Take it into a new folder or new sketch. And then save it as a down counter switch. Now what I do here is along with this to switch once this to liquidation, I live near a variable called college, which by default is zero. And know what I'm going to do is probably you might have understood it very well till now. So Ipswich one expressed what I will do. It's. Count clusters. Cyril, the French count equal to then Lord Byron Ellen Count and Delia Thompson. So the count will be incremented and will be printed on the serial port and the of thousand resistance. Similarly, we will do it from minus. The only thing we have to make sure about minus minus is you don't want to see values. Then you do. So I'll just do this. If count is less than zero counted.Zero. This is a single line. If condition.

Therefore, you can skip the limit. Remember, if there are multiple lines and if condition, then you have to have the opening entries. But if it is a single condition, you can skip that. So my program is done. Let's see the output. So I will upload it into the system now and we'll try to see. Again. It will see here. It's important. You don't want all the counts to be implemented by two times in a single switch. So you may want to add the pulling effect to you. It's called it's pulling when you on purpose, stall the microcontroller. Stop the microcontroller from doing other things. It's only. I have not done any polling here. So let's see, because I have Ed 1/2, which is usually sufficient to move my finger on the switch. Now I clicked it once and found this one. I click it another thing. Counties to actually get one more thing down the street. Now I'm a little bit pressed, so if I came in president with a delay of 1/2, the count will keep incrementing. See released nine Prestwich to become 6543217. After that, it might have gone into the negative headlines, but it won't because now we have redone it that if it was less than zero, then the conceivable. And then you can increment it like this. Now, this is just one example.

45

In the same way you can have an LCD declared, make it on here, make it off here, make it. Any number of GPI goes on and off in this if conditions off switch for this. You can also make something like if digital switch 1% and 4%. If digital data switched to just like that, you can mix and match those conditions. But for this session, I will not add those complexities because I don't want you to be scared about it in the percentage. So this is the basic switch interface. I hope you will be able to do this. The sites. Please try to follow the bread tutorial that I'm going to add into the section. They were shot almost ten years ago, but they are. I think this should be sufficient for you to get an idea of how to interface with the breadboard. If you already know about the breadboard, then you skip the lessons. But if much. There is nothing to. There is no harm in deflation.

SWITCHING CIRCUIT - DC LOAD SWITCHING

Hi. Now that we have understood how we can interface and input with SB 32. Now let's turn this turn some of the switching subjects which can be used to interface a wide variety of awkward devices. Now, when it comes to connecting different devices, we have to understand one thing very clearly, and that is when you when you create an integer rich and output on it has to be 32, it is either 3.3 which monitors zero. Now, this is a very small voltage that can be generated. And with this one voltage, all you can run on directly is either an entity or maybe a buzzer or something like that. But nothing more than that. So there can be primarily two different types of switch and circuits that might be needed. One is called as DC switching circuits means a DC load switching. And the other one, I call it an AC load switching. Now in this project we will try to understand the DC switching. Then we will try to understand the easy load switching. And then we'll try to do some kind of some list of lines as far as supporting part is concerned. All we need to do is we need to make up in high or low. So here the understanding part is on the soft side is on the electronics side and not much on the programming switch. So let's see now, when you said we see, what does it mean this enormous anything that works on this. It can be a motor. It can be a big blizzard. It can be big. It is volatilities and things like that. So any of those kind of circuits can directly not be switched on using the 3.304. That's like what we use speed something or that's transistor switching, rather straight switching circuits. It's actually very simple to understand. That's why I'm not going to give you any detailed notes on it, but I'll keep these notes on the presentation so that you can access them. So this is a transistor switching circuit. A lawyer is usually connected. From the supply voltage. Let's call it V. S. Now this supply voltage can be any wattage which goes on to sleep. Maybe the load it's firework one, so here will be fireworks. If the law is a 12 volt motor or relay on anything like that or buzzer, then this will be 12. So this this is not dependent upon to use it, but it is dependent upon the law. Positive of the law should go to this and the negatives should go to.

In return of this ambient transistor should be grounded. And this shouldn't be given a small value. That's the stuff. So small that the current passing through this base on eBay. Which we guidance should be less than or equal to 10 million. Now we are going to generate 3.3 work here. So 3:30 a.m. will allow maximum 10 million gallons per inch to flow to this register towards the base. So when you make this feel high or one. Usually at 3.3, Walt Whitman made the 700. Let's see what happens. Whenever you generate 3.3 was on this. The best actor and best we would report the generations that followed best and the large collective that includes from the law from the Vegas, through the law, through the transistor towards ground. And the law in thumb turns on. Maybe we could zero the junction. Somebody would last on the north for best and therefore the load turns. Simple as that. Nothing much complicated in it. The complication or the design considerations?Strong.

Transistorized Switching

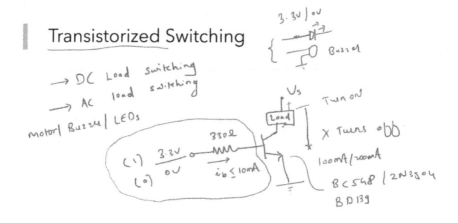

When you try to understand how much is the current flowing through this look. Because as you can see, the load has to pass this current to the strongest body. So if your load is taking, let's say, 100 or 200 million gallons. Then you can use any simple transistor like sci fi footage. On.20 904. Anything like that because they allow them excluded with the entry of current to pass through it. Now let us consider that we have had a bigger law that extends the mean something at 12 volt and one MVA. So that's not and that gives this kind of funds to not annually to go for a bigger power transition funds to make really monthly that are excellent you know something like that. So the choice of transistor depends upon the choice of route. Apart from that here, nothing else will change. You can use any input transistor to perform or to create a switching circuit like this. It's simply just doesn't matter. What is your load as long as you have used for as long as you have selected this light transistor to be used with it. This is debatable. Translates with you about the socket for this. This is the socket footage.

RELAY SWITCHING CIRCUIT WITH ESP32

Hi. Now that we have tried to understand the theory behind intricacy in the really. Now let's try to see some of it in action. So I'm following this exact schematic over here that translates to messaging. So it is created onto this interesting board, if you can see. So here we have a transistor, then a small in addition to the store combo. Then there is an additional instrument you can see which is going to the base of transistor. Then here I have really and here is a terminal which is the return and C command. And so the one beneath the red is gone and the rightmost one. And as you can see, I'm following this exact circuit over here. If you can see here, then this is a tube in a C cable. If I just show it to you completely. So this is my. A cable. And here one point of the cable. As you can see in the schematic is going to the relay contact here. The other point of the relay contact, it's going to. But this is the bulb. Okay. And the other point of the bulb is then going to. The AC cable itself. So AC these are the two points of one point of the going to really other point of delivering the AC cable. And the other point, obviously cable going back to exactly what we have seen here. And I also happen to have a bulb connected to this. I have connected this spin over here. Which has been a virtual arrangement to the base of Transistor. And a very simple, little blinking program. It's in action. Now, let's see the requirements to involve one which is provided on this supply. If you don't have this one or if you don't have any such kind of interests involved, then you can easily obtain the readily available related to this box which comes in markets. Let me show you that in a moment. Logic and see here, this is a single module. Something like this will be easily available in local markets. Focus.

!lay Switching Circuit

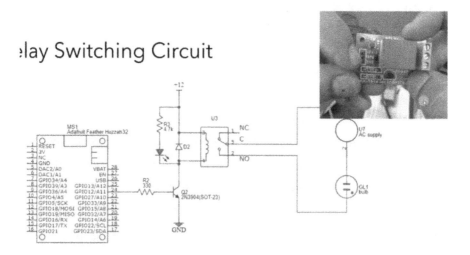

So it has got a 12 volt input line. Then this input this should be coming from microcontroller and this is the granted. So this is a single channel really model. I'll give you the same thing here. You can see an order them here and set it down here. The middle one is onwards and then the similar base. You may also find a two channel delay module for the channel delay module on any system. The logic underlying logic remains the same. Now, what I've done is I have simply used a small blinking program on the budget. If you look at the code here now, let's try to download this code and then. Let's see the output. When the code is downloaded, you can also start hitting the pixel three. I'm not sure if that will be audible from this distance of microphone, but let's see now. The code has been compiled. And it's uploaded. Now the program has been uploaded into the. Bold. Now. Let's see if it works. Now, if you see here's this spot power indication, it's on off. And I'm going to stick my microphone near to the rear. You may hear the sound of picking clear my name, but it not coming on off, however. Let's make some changes. It's not that long ago. It's nothing. You have to remember very well that it's this line of life going to be here. So if you are quoting you all the above, make sure you do not touch anything over here. And before I want to do is I just use the in 60 seconds. Once it gets too fast off switch

50

immediately. When it comes to switching plugs, the might sometimes give them for the purpose of simplicity and also using a small delta so that all these sort of innovations can be carried out very easy. We are also planning to switch the symbol on and off to Alexa. So the circuits and my setup is going to remain the same. Now I'm going to connect this to main spot supply and I'm going to start. So that as you can see with the reliance on. You have the audible feedback from here. But it is all. Getting it. Now I'll take the microphone back to my column that it should belong. Really?Just a moment. Okay.

Now, this is my in transit as it looks like. Now one thing is here, I'm using external power supply, 12 volt power on this into this board. So you also have to make sure the ground of is Win32 and this socket is very common, as you can see through this green line. Anyhow, if you are interfacing a board, a small signal memory like this, then it will have coiled voltage. Right then inputs and the ground builds. So here. Because. The ground should be made of common materials that have to do ground as well as transport. And they should be coming from controllers. I would stay here with you. We will be using the same setup. Maybe we will have some other prints, but we're using the same setup whenever we are experimenting with triplets.

READING CAPACITIVE TOUCH INPUTS ON ESP32

We'll try to see how we can see on how we can utilize the capacitive touch screens on iOS. We touch ID, you can use them to turn on or off any particular load, or you can also use them as switch inputs. Instead of applying or using physical buttons, you can use them as menu buttons for identity and you can use them for. Any such proposals. Okay. So for this experiment, all I'm going to have is a single ESD 32 federal 32 board. Basically, this is an absolute was up in the 32 board, which is based on USP 32 and I'm going to use a single pin. Female Two female connectors over here. So it has got. Female So the male two male connectors because what we connect on one inch as well as on the other and on the softer side, I'm going to use the E and I'm going to use another software to make it interesting, which is called S terminal by the. C-Terminal by Brie. This is interesting. Yes, of course, Arduino has a built in serial monitor, but I just want to see things in a different way. That's why I'm asking you to download this software. It's a very simple utility. I'm going to chart single file that you can download and start to use. This is basically the serial terminal replacements. So usually on a development computer, this it's so useful utility that I keep it on my desktop almost all the. So this is terminal. We are going to use this for what? I'll show you. Meanwhile, let's get back to. We told you. So with this photo, if you look at the pin now, we have so many touch inputs that that's zero, that's six, nine, that's three, that's aged at 70 my vegetables.

How to accept capacitive touch on esp32 Feather Board (touchread)

ADAFRUIT HUZZAH32 PIN DIAGRAM

- 14
- 32
- 15
- 33
- 27
- 12
- 13
- 4

So all in all, the number 1432, 15, 33, 27, 12, 13 and then before, these are the touch inputs which we have on the industrial tools output due to board. Now if you have to use any of them, all you need to do is simply use a function called touch you. How does this function looks like to see that? First of all, I just took a blank sketch. Let's do a wild setup. And definitely we can also be doing what we do and saying to score adds capacitive touch inputs. Let's begin. Zero.Zero. And here what I'm going to do is let's stick a project of Alexa in the call to Dutch attitude and just give up in them. So we have all indispensable connections, like CEOs. Say, pin number 14 on the board in number 14 is here. So that's already been number 14 cereal. Don't put in an egg and then you stick a small do you. Okay. Thousand millisecond so that we have some time duration between two inputs. Now if you look at it carefully, I'm not sure whether it focuses well or not, but this it's a C, I and this is been number for. So I have been number 14 over here, to which I'm connecting a single wire. Okay. What's the problem here? Let me look at my coach. Okay. It has not got any collusive tax on capital here. So let's upload it again. Meanwhile, I have this one wire over here, as you can see, connected to pin number four pin. After the code is downloaded, we will open the cereal terminal and will try to attach this particular flash with you. And we needed to know what is the difference between the different touches that we may have. Remember, when everything is in capacitive touch input like this, you will have to estimate the same manner that I'm doing. Legacy when nothing is trashed here. The value that is coming on the Syrian port, it's 62, 63, something like that.

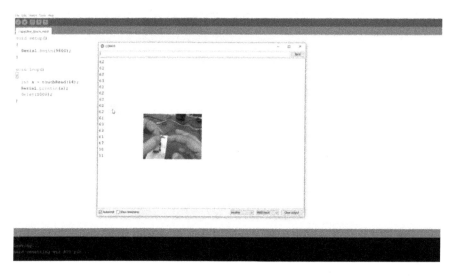

Now I'm going to just gently give it a touch. I touched it and you see the value dropped down to 31 something. I raised my finger. 64, 64, 64, something that's stuck in the velodrome stop. Okay. So 64 AIDS or about 60, it's something that you don't touch. And below 40, it's something you touch. See here. As simple as that. So the testing is done so easily. Why? I wanted to ask if we just should. Okay. We don't do the software. We have a serial plotter here also in our dinners. So I'm just wanting to have a little fun here. I'm not going to give any delay. So what will happen is will get data very fast, but I'm still terminal and I want to plot them. So I showed you about Terminal by Billy, but it's okay if you don't download that because we have a serial slaughtering tools also since usually I used to use the terminal, maybe we show you that softer as well after this one step. Now the touch is being read and send on the input first. This is really. So if I just open serial plotter, you'll see these are the values we're getting them continuously.

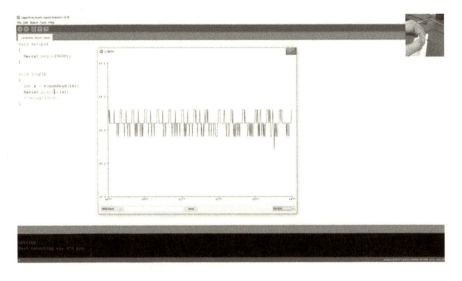

Now, if I touch it. See. That's it. That's it. That's it. It's very easily visualizing. The Syrian border is moving dynamically very fast. So I'll just stop. Serial plotter. And since we have downloaded, let's do this. So the company we have, it's content. And what we want to do is we want to simply create a graph. Now let's connect. For some reason. It just crashed just a moment ago. Okay. It's up to this question. Nevertheless, I hope you got the idea over here with serial plots. So if I catch. Even the Bible is in my hand, because if I touch even the blood from outside, that is supposed to do that. As you can see. Okay. Now, I'll just keep it like this the way it is now here on the breadboard. It's just a gentle touch. And the valuable strong.Now, if you want to turn on or off or devices and things, then just do watch more. In addition to school built in, come off outputs here instead of even serially printing it. What I do is. If it is less than 40 and digital ride quality and also built in common higher health and digital lives and the d underscore built in coma it wins. What if the if the touch input that is delayed or recorded is less than 40 then. I want to turn the LCD on otherwise and it should be turned off. Now let's try to see this in action. So he and I have. Code is been downloaded. I think it's done. Now that's the spirit. And you see that the difference is noticeable. Just let's stick it to you. Dutch. Dutch, Dutch. At Symbolisms.

Now in this way you can use all the available touch inputs on iOS with touch ID. What are the other inputs available to you? You have all this and personally, at least on the Fed that are due to world. If you have any other use 52 compatible balls then it may have more for us. We have one, two, three, four, five, six, seven, eight prints over here which can be used as touch inputs.

DHT22 SENSOR INTERFACING WITH ESP32

Let's start to see some actual sensor interfacing with ISP such as, you know, the primary purpose, primary motive of discourse is to learn Internet of Things or IAG applications and therefore having sensor values which we can sense or intermarriage or to some other place is a vital part of discourse. Let's start now. There are different types of sensors available and depending upon how much you have already done in embedded systems, you can correlate with this things. Although I'll give a perspective of a compute pressures. If you have some experience, then you are easily able to understand and even give you a couple of depressions. It's particularly for you, but don't worry. So there are basically two type of sensors which you went to visit microcontrollers. One is called as an analog sensor, which can view a specified voltage, which relates to the applied analog input. For example, there is a temperature sensor called 1135 which gives an millivolts 30 degrees Celsius. So if my room temperature currently is 25 degrees Celsius, it will give an output of 50 me which to interface microcontroller with this kind of sensors. What we need is to use an E to convert an analog to digital converter which can convert this value into a particular digital output, which then can be used to understand the sensor value and perform the relative or required operations based on which. Then there are digital sensors. Digital sensors also come in different types, and the most popular or the most simplest one is something called that's of very basic one zero output sensor. So I will not be covering the sensors because they are pretty straightforward to use. So there can be a fired sensor, there can be a sound sensor, there can be any such kind of sensor which does that. It gives an output of logic. One when they send something or output of logic zero and they don't send some to be. Air sensor is also one such thing which can be used to detect the presence of a human body inside a room or something like that. And then comes. The most interesting part was the sensors, which gives digital data over some kind of protocol. Maybe they give you data on protocols like IPC, or maybe they give you data in terms of the rate of the signal, like ultrasonic sensors and others are going to send some sense of it. You spit out you. Now for the scope of this project, I am particularly not going to cover the analog inputs and it is a reason for which I hope you will be able to relate with that. And the reason is the analog input. Obviously 32 are not that well documented. You will be disturbed, you will be confused by looking at a lot of different tutorials online. So some of them will see it will read from 0 to 3.3, some of them will see it will read from 0 to 1.1 volt. And most importantly, even if you figured out all the documentations and understand how to use it, the end result is the easy to do to analog. It spins up nonlinear so you will not be able to differentiate between different digits. Very remote. It is okay to use analog input for academic projects or just for the studies case, but that's out of the scope of this project. I want you to understand this better to do and start computing industrial grade project as well. So my ideal suggestion is if you all want to use an analog input, then please go and use some the external in this picture for the scope of this project. I'm not going to include analog voltages, but I will keep adding different projects on use with what you do in the project as well as on the YouTube channel, which will showcase how we can interface with different sensors now. But in the scope of this project, I'm going to use the HD to do temperature and humidity sensor. The reason being first, it is very easy to interface with DSP.

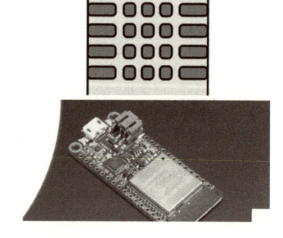

DHT22

Interfacing with ESP32

And the second thing is it is very easily available across the world. It is cheaper and we usually get it. Almost every is modular. If you look at the popularity of the istituto, you can see the official tutorials of lot provided by Microsoft, Azure and Amazon. This also includes this one sensor with controller which can demonstrate the details sending onto the cloud. So let's try to understand the Institute for this use. So I have this two sensors with me currently. One is called DSD two and the blue one, which you can see here. It's called SDH two. And it is I'm just going to show this to you for comparison. So the issue two looks like this white big one, and the B is two. And when it's smaller, usually we don't use the estimate of an audience because it is not so accurate. The range of sensing is also not so good and therefore these 2 to 2, it's kind of the standard thing to use. Now how you can use the issue to do, let's try to understand some basic specifications first. So it has a very wide operating temperature range out of the sensing range. I would see that it's from -40 degrees Celsius. It can zero 200% of humidity. It works on 3 to 6 volt operating voltage and it has a very good resolution of the reading defense.

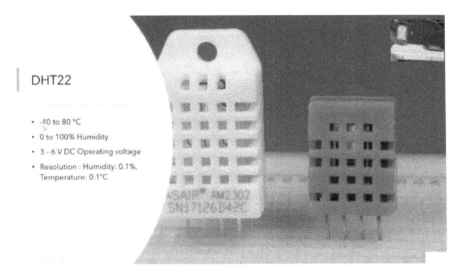

DHT22

- -40 to 80 °C
- 0 to 100% Humidity
- 3 - 6 V DC Operating voltage
- Resolution : Humidity: 0.1%, Temperature: 0.1°C

Moreover, the connection of the issue to two is also very simple. If you look at it, this is actually a module. Okay, so the sensor itself is a four wire sensor. As you can see over here in this image, it looks focused. Not now, me. So it looks like this. Which has got to be number one, two, three, four. Then number one is sick.

DHT22 Pinout

- Pin 1 → 3.3v
- Pin 2 → GPIO with 10k Pullup
- Pin 3 → NC
- Pin 4 → GND

And number two is data three is not connected. And for this count, the number two, that is data. It can go to any of the three to you and get pulled up. So the schematic, if you want it, should be looking like this. If you get just the sense this one, then you need to create a schematic like this. But what I have here is a module. Now let me just get closer to it so we can focus it. So on the model, if you check, focus. You can see there are only three points ground zero and data and the required full up resistor is all readily available. With you. So depending upon if you're getting a module or if you are getting a particular sensor directly, the sensor texel you have to choose which you want to go for. Now, let me make the connections first so that it becomes easier for us to start experimenting. So here I inserted into the Mississippian the attainment. And I'm going to connect it to. 3.3. So I have some. Male to male. Female to male bias here to make my life easier. And I connected it to 2.3% or not. I'm going to use another combination of male female to create a larger wire. And this one I will use as the tap in. I'm going to connect the deep up into I'm going to really connect it to energy by you. But I'm particularly using the spin a lot.

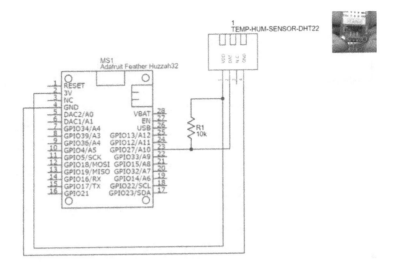

So it's the ACL fault in. So to do so, just leave me connected to working. Basically it doesn't matter actually that you connected so they could be number 40 and I'm connecting it to. No. I mean, so it is a seal and steer seal in this. It's forbidden. And lastly, I want to connect account here. So make sure when you are using devices or connections, then try to keep your writing simple so that you can understand which. I don't have much good advice here. As a luxury much of my body is to do to since it is not connected. Once you have the issue to two connected. All you need to do is to install some libraries in order to get to the sensor and display the values on. That's what we are going to do now. So the two libraries you're going to need is to send celebrity by the throat and a unified sensibility. Now, let's. Let's test the waters. So let's open our Dino. And here, let me just stick a new sketch. Completely new one. And I will save it as the HD to do. Yes. I'm just going to call it as the istitutoest and let's try to see the output of which first of all, do auto sketch include liability and manage litigants. Here, you will have to search for the celebrities with jobs to do so. One of the best is in celebrity by the fruit and fruit universe and celebrity. So the HD, I just type HD and look at all the BSD related libraries available. As a part of experimentation, you are free to use any of the libraries also. I'm going to use a of libraries because I am using data from smaller. So this is the issue isn't celebrity married approach. Just install. Nothing. It is also asking you that it depends on unified sense of liability.

So better if we have a chat itself and all. So we have installed the BSD as well as any parts and celebrity. Now simply go to find. Examples. Here you will find the installed library. So enough root beer stews and celebrity. Unless Sydney is stupid. Now I'm going to complete this score completely over here in my test score. Let's simplify things a bit. Okay. Let me just remove the unwanted comment first. So that becomes easier for us to understand. You can anyways go to the documentation later on. So this is the step in and this is the history type. And then there are just the values being read. Each is humidity followed by its temperature. I don't want any of the stuff coming in here and just want to print it. Okay, so let's keep it simple. So humidity is X percentage and then temperature, it's the next degree Celsius. Nothing else that we want to keep.Index. Nothing. Nothing. Nothing. And let's just have a of those events. So it was already there in the beginning of the call. So all we need to do is download this score where I have connected the distances that I just need to mention that number. So it is. For billion, for sure. So let's put the strap in to be one for Ambien, then. So you can really function here. All we have is this tool functions which will enable us to read the temperature as well as humidity from the sensor. So let's try to upload this code now and see the object. The code is being compiled. Sometimes you may get impatient sometimes about the operating of. How did the downloading process with you is with attitudes a little bit definitely slower as compared to the regularity the books. Now the completion is almost about to be done and we'll start uploading the code into the board and then we'll be able to see the output. Exploring now. Connecting, writing and acting, writing. Directing.Done. It's possible, but.

Nothing. It is not able to do anything. You need to be prepared with this also. Now, this is a problem and I am not going to commit to this moment. I'm not going to edit this with you because this is going to happen with most of us. We cannot to be too sensitive for the first time. We may not get the output correctly. We may get something wrong. Something is mistaken. So what do you have to do here is you have to check for the power cables correctly and then also check the data being been connected correctly. Also, I have Mr. French a new line here, so I will do that. And meanwhile, I'll keep checking, dividing. Now, as you can see now, I have made some changes. Okay. Identically installed the sensor on the board. And just that it's some visual library, which I'm not able to connect to the screen very well. So what I've done is I'm using PIN number 27 now, and now I can see the output. Now, this is a very simple experiment. You can also try to increase the humidity by doing something they put on to it. If you can see the humidity increase to 78, 83. If you do and the temperature is the temperature is basically the room temperature. If I have no small and so it let's see if it changes the temperature of it. Not much change the impression, I would say, but my camera lens is a little bit cheaper because it is on for some time. So let me touch it with the camera and let me see if I can notice some change, some sensing elements inside. So you will have to have heart it going through this. So therefore it is a very perfect candidate for sensing the room temperature and humidity inside your house. So this is the institute. So you might want to make changes according to your core. Now I'm connecting it here on V number 27 and now the breadboard connection between the seven is looking. But also my sense it is a bit old. Maybe it was not connecting well with the wires, so I have directly mounted it on to the bridge. Now this is how you can get the humidity and temperature values to be a strict sensor. But this is just the start of or beginning of the stored. Similarly, there can be a number of different sensors which can be used. So this is a very simple sound sensor. As I said, it simply gives logical one or zero. And this is a proximity sensor. It gives one output logic, one of logic zero whenever you put the hand in front of it. And then there are a number of different sensors which can be used to get different values. What we are going to do is we are going to give you setups on one is the 2 to 2 sensor and the other one is this are able and using this two setups, we will be performing a number of different experiments that are related to lot.

ESP32 WEATHER MONITORING OVER WIFI (LAN)

We have seen how we can perform a device control in the LAN. So I just thought of keeping this with you. Immediately after that, we do the weather monitoring using data in LAN, just like last project. Also, this video cord has been taken from random note audience. Please visit their website. They have quite a lot many different tutorials on use with a two on here. I have taken this code to make it simplified for all equals takers so that it should be easier for you to experiment on the Istituto and UC computer. The concept is completely similar. The only thing that has changed now is previously here we had a delay. Now here we have a new to 2%. So we have already understood about the issue to to censor. It looks like this.

Concept

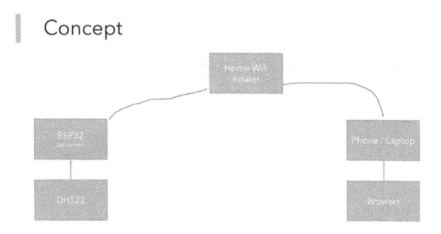

It actually looks like it's just a forbidden connector. You can buy it as a model or as an individual sensor and you connect it to the.

DHT22 Pinout

- Pin 1 → 3.3v
- Pin 2 → GPIO with 10k Pullup
- Pin 3 → NC
- Pin 4 → GND

Yes, we touch it, too. Just like this. So pin number one should go to table number two is due to pin, which should go to image of go in in GPO 27. This data should look weird up to here. This is important because the output of this sensor, it's open, Jim. If it don't pull it up externally, it will not show any voltage levels, either one or zero. But that's an issue.

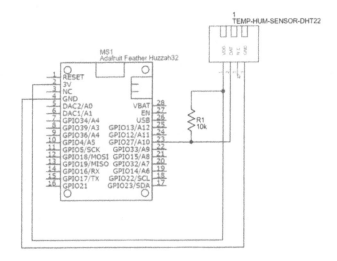

Pull it up. It will get zero levels properly indicator when the battery is NC and the number four needs to connect to ground just like previous project in this one. Also, we need to add two libraries to already know since we have already read them. I will with that step and I'm pretty sure you have already seen the previous project.

Required Libraries

- AsyncTCP - - Download here
- ESPAsyncWebserver -- Download here
- DHT Sensor Library by Adafruit
- Adafruit Unified Sensor Library
- Program files → Arduino (x86) → Libraries

So we want to have this used to send celebrity matter fruit. We want to have the unified sense of library also. So all of these things are already done there. So I'm not going to repeat them over here. So let's directly open our camera and jumpstart into the action and see how this one goal works and what changes we can do in the and save this score. Does land issue to do with me? Open my camera here again. So as you can see, just to make things interesting, what I have done is I'm adding a certain amplitude, so I'm not going to touch it with soldering on, but I'll just keep it a bit close by so that I can blow some hot air into it.

So if I keep it like this and if I. Alison Caldwell Alright then, I'm pretty sure that the issue will get a bit hotter. So the court is here again, the same changes. All you need to do is you need to just add your life insurance right over here. And then you need to mention the type of system that I'll just make to simplify and remove the unnecessary comment. So we have the issue to do connected to PIN number 27 and these are my last conventions, no other changes required for the schools. So let's upload this and see the output for this output. Also, we will either use a mobile browser or a computerized process. Let's. And the court had started compiling. And I know you know that it's it's quite slow, many of them. So let's wait here for some time. The uploading had started now. So let the record get uploaded completely and then will open the Syrian terminal that will see the IP address. Assange.Connecting to a fire.Connecting to a fire, connecting to find the IP. All we need to do again, just like last time it's copy this IP address. Open a browser and paste it over here. As you can see, there is a temperature and humidity value coming over here. But if I just try to do some experiment with just the.Gives. You can see the temperature is 27.70. Refresh it. It's getting hotter. 21. Okay, so I have. Mm hmm. So this is the camera. This is what I'm doing here. So I'm just putting a heart. So then close to it, not touching it.Just closed, which. Okay. Make sure you if you do these exercises, be careful. Now you can see the temperature is 29. It is rising slowly. If I blow it, actually, it will reduce the temperature because of the cold air coming out of the smoke. If you have a hot air gun, it's much better. You can directly demonstrate. You can directly blossom some hot air over here. Unfortunately, I don't have one now, so I'm following something. We are vectors like this, but the points. I'm distraught, I guess. Every one of you. The temperature is rising. Am if I now kipyegon back in the counselor up to the sled with the salting gun holder, then you can see the temperature will start dropping now. 31.60 then. Not much doubt. 31.50. So on.

And so again, not to mention this time as well, what you can do is you can use a mobile browser also. But it's not visible. So we need to do it very dark in order for it to be okay. The fresh. 31.2 refresh to 1.1. 30.9. So I have taken this two experience, particularly from an and I'm notorious and I thought they could be interesting to be added in the project maybe a study.

WHAT IS INTERNET OF THINGS

Hi. Let's get started. By taking a total understanding of what exactly is Internet of Things and what are the fundamentals of it. Now, since this is the primary agenda of the schools, that is to understand the Iot, it is important for us to have a clear understanding about the fundamentals of Iot, and that's what we are going to achieve in this particular project. So let's get started. Now, when we say Iot or when you say Internet of Things, what are the things that should come in our minds primarily? And if we think about it in this way, the Internet of Things, it's primarily sensing the information from a moment. Now, when I say a moment, it's a very broader context. The environment can be of a simple role. An involvement can be an industrial involvement or an industrial machinery or something. The involvement which we have to sense can be jungle or atmospheric, whether it can be an entire building. It can be a running vehicle. It can be almost anything. Wherever you can connect a sensor that becomes an environment or that particular location for your departure, it can be what? It can be your energy meter. It can be a completed building's building management system. Can do almost anything. The primary thing, it's the environment from where you are sensing the information and this information when you sensitive in a conventional context, what we do is we simply display somewhere locally using a display. But in Iot, the purpose is basically to transfer this information to an Internet based location somewhere on the Internet where we want to store this information. And what's the purpose of storing this information on Internet? The purpose is very simple. We want to perform some kind of data analysis and insights, try to find out some insights on this information. Now, why? To send it on Internet? The reason is, again, very simple, because once you send the information to Internet, you can be anywhere in the world and you can still access the information. So I may very well have my house in one part of the world, and I may be and I can be very easily able to look at the parameters in my house from another continent. Same can apply for a vehicle which is running in Europe and I want to have a complete view of how it is going. Where is my transport going when it is being well, where it is being completely offloaded or where it can be, but it is moving in the location. I can monitor that sitting in India or something like that. So gathering information from an informant, sending it over the Internet to perform some data analysts, why we perform the dialysis so that we can make better decisions about our business, about our system, about our home. I'm going to my home right now, and it's a very hot summer day.

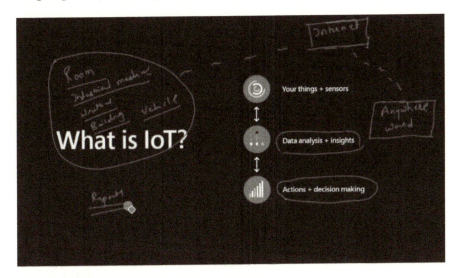

So what I want to do is my air conditioning unit should be done on 10 minutes before I go to home so that no limits call out. Simple as that. It's a very simple consumer electronic application. On the other hand, if you want to see the analytics of a production plant sitting in your office, which is located in probably another city, then also Iot can be helpful in gathering the intent of production information and create field reports about the production for you. The applications of Iot are not figuratively, not just as a matter of speech, but literally limitless. There is almost no limits to what you can do with Internet of Things. So as I said, there are things from which you gather the information. These things are sensors, actuators, some microprocessor microcontroller units, which can do the information from there, some connectivity to which it can send the information or the data to some Internet based sources.

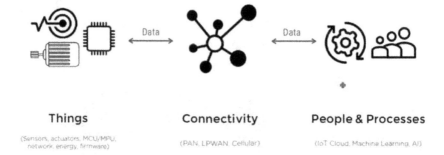

Things

(Sensors, actuators, MCU/MPU,
network, energy, firmware)

Connectivity

(PAN, LPWAN, Cellular)

People & Processes

(IoT Cloud, Machine Learning, AI)

And then you process that information in a very simple format. And this is how I would like to explain on this. I would like to outline I know the most important part of this entire picture is the thing itself. That is the first point of that is the first you can see the starting point of an idea application is ting. Ting means the environment from which you are reading the information. The first point of hard of that electronic part of it which senses the information and some sort of work of cloud. This usually is consisting of this primal blocks, as you can see. So there can be input sensors and variety of different forms. There can be output devices like the air conditioning unit. I'll give you an example which needs to turn on and off. Then there is a controller which has to process this information and using the network interface, the controller will then send this information over to Internet. So this is about external communication.

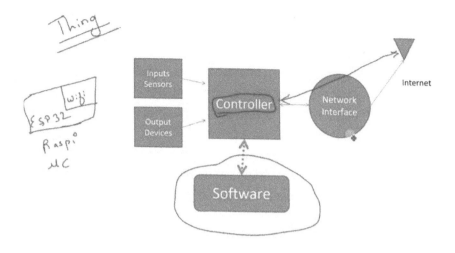

It will send the required information, it will assume the required information and then perform some unknown action. If there is not enough action involved, then it will simply keep reading the input values from the sensors and logging it onto the internet. So and to do all these things, this controller request a complete piece of reconfigurable software embedded into it. So this in a very general purpose format, you can see as one part or the endpoint of your thing. Now here the controller can be DSP 32. The controller can be a complete, sophisticated system like Raspberry Pi or a very basic microcontroller. It can be any such thing. The reason why we prefer ESP 32is because it comes with onboard capability of connecting to Wi-Fi, and it is also low cost. Raspberry Pi also comes with life, but the cost is not suitable or justifiable for a single unit for us, in the sense that if you have to create so is better, to do therefore is the best and ideal candidate to perform this particular kind of system. Now, the question here is, first of all, what are the network interfaces we are talking about? Why is it the only network interface that is used? And I are definitely not. See, the point here is we want to do what I do is just have one more slide over here. So that I can give this information. So the point primarily it's. Just a minute. We want information that is coming from some sources to be sent over to cloud. Now it can take different groups to reach that position. To give you an example, in one of my project, what we did was all the sensors were connected via a Zigbee protocol. Because my if I was not available. And there were number of sensors. This is one sensitive tool. And Alexis and all this information is collected at one location. And that one location was having a computer. Through the interface. It was receiving the information and then the computer was sending the information out. My lab. Now this is one topology. In a practical situation, you can correct any number of such topologies, maybe everywhere. Why, Orlan may not be possible. In that case, the controller chips like the photon can also be used, which comes with the capability of directly connecting a SIM card, which now becomes a SIM card. Connected connectivity. What happens? You can leverage the inability of a similar internet facility and directly connect to cloud. So wi fi is one option. LAN is another option. Bluetooth is also used sometimes. Zigbee is also used and very popular. Currently Lora is also being used now by Lora is getting popular because you can send larger or you can send information over larger distances, a much less power use in Europe. So if you have a coal mine or something which is located at a remote location that is no internet connectivity like this, then you cannot see as Lora. However, this is not the point of current discussion. Currently, we are assuming that we are having ESP 32with why. If I don't do it and we are trying to understand how we can build lot systems based on it, but since we are starting here, so my job to give you an overview of all the available things which are present out there. Now, as stated before, the applications are literally limitless, primarily where we work or when I primarily work. Is this for various consumers industrial, commercial and infrastructure. But as I said, there are a number of different applications, which also includes variables as well.

Applications

- Consumer
- Industrial
- Commercial
- infrastructure

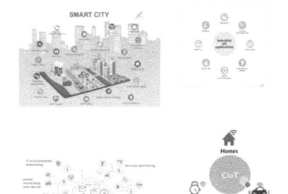

That's connected cars, connected buildings, hospitals, connected manufacturing and many things. Now, what are the requirements of a proper Iot architecture? The most important requirement of an IP architecture. When you are creating your next project, it's whatever you design. It should be able to handle the proper hardware and software heterogeneity if possible. And I'm saying if possible, it should have a single or not more than two different programming languages. And all all the hardware should be easily talking, using the software with each of the your hardware, whatever you select, should be reliable and scalable so that even if you are creating one system or if you have lives of 10,000 systems, it should be able to handle it. The data latency is one point which comes into the picture, but we will discuss later latency later. Some applications may require a very immediate response or a very limited data vision, but most of theIot applications are not hard. Real-Time Systems A little bit of small delay in data transmission is always the important thing is the architecture should be secured by design because in the end it is going to be an IP protocol and IP protocols or anything that is going on Internet is Heikkinen.

IoT Architecture Requirements

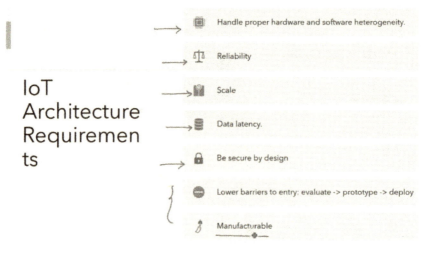

Handle proper hardware and software heterogeneity.

Reliability

Scale

Data latency.

Be secure by design

Lower barriers to entry: evaluate -> prototype -> deploy

Manufacturable

So if you're design is by by the design itself, if your system is secure, then you can minimize those kind of threats. Lastly, if you are using or creating battery operated systems, the power consumption is important and if it is a microcontroller based system you are creating, it should be manufactured and built. Not every project that you create are required to be manufactured. For example, if a company comes to me asking they want do they want to implement smart manufacturing in their industry, then I don't need a manu facturable solution. I need a custom built solution which is suitable for Dutch company. But tomorrow, if a customer comes to you and asks for a home, a safety monitoring system which can have a prediction, it's going to have gas leak inspection, fire detection, those kind of things. Then it has to be a manu facturable system. So there are two ways to implement and I would approach. One is when you are creating project and another one is when you are creating products. I'll discuss that later on in something. So there are different technologies involved. One is examining then communications protocols which are involved. And then there are a variety of different hydrous. Why are Europeans of Korea is very lucrative.

Technologies Involved

→ Programming in

C / C++

Python

Web development (all web tech)

Machine Learning

Cloud software

Data analysis

App development

→ Protocols

Data sending from device to Cloud

HTTP

MQTT

→ Hardware

Microcontroller

Sensors

Devices

That is. It is simply because usually you will not find a single person who is good in hardware as well as communication with the girls as well as with them. Therefore, if you muster the skill, you become a very valuable asset in terms of employment as well as you become a valuable resource as a supplier of AI systems. What you want to do eventually is choice show. But my job is to explain you the benefits of becoming good. I. Now, when I say you want to send information to cloud, what do I mean by that? So by nature, you're going to have two different types of cloud service. One is, if you haven't heard about it, Louis or Google Cloud or Microsoft as well, something like that. So these are major custom designs with major cloud providers. You need to take this approach when you are creating a product. You cannot afford to use in a pure psychotic or as variety hub when you are creating a single person. When you are creating a single project. This is Colette's platform as a service when you are creating a single project. The recommended way is to use software as a service product that a number of different software as a service platforms which are maybe made IAP platforms. All you have to do is create an account over there, then start to start sending data out of there. The visualizations are really analytics obviously, and all you need to do is simply configure them and spell your requirements and spell your needs. Now, throughout the project of this particular project, we will have more focus on the suspect, because this kind of this kind of budgets are easy to create, quick to learn, and suitable for most of the project requirements, and also gives an insight about how you will create the product when the time comes for each. So these are the primarily two different choices of cloud service bus allsorts. Not much option in bus. Yes, of course there are, but they're not limited to 5 to 10 different options. So and you will eventually end up in something that is standard like Amazon on IBM or Microsoft will cloud. But when it comes to choosing a softer, just sort of the spectrum, then there is a ton of choice. Literally, there will be 50 plus different options available. I'm just giving you some names simply as a reference. So the thing works, is there everything? Is there sense of cloud device, cloud things? Big numerics out of all these things can speak, is a very, very powerful platform and it is also available for you to evaluate and not only to evaluate. Three You can also do a project on things speak which can be in production for quite some time or quite long.

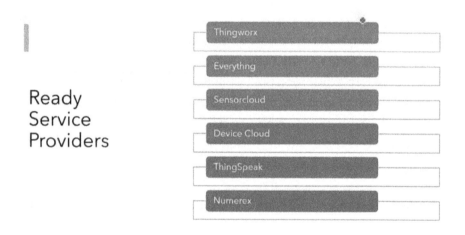

Ready
Service
Providers

Thingworx

Everythng

Sensorcloud

Device Cloud

ThingSpeak

Numerex

So this is a very what are you going to see or what have you off? How are you this distance? What are the different cloud options available? What are the IRP projects? What are the products? I just kind of hinge when you would use suspect form and then use cross-platform.

IOT PROTOCOLS AND THINGSPEAK

We'll try to see some protocols which are used in creation, fire resistance. And we'll also try to see one of the platforms which we will be using to create lot based product or activist project. In our project. There are actually like many different protocols involved in creation of a single system. But for the simplicity, what we are doing here is we are assuming that we have a network connected device like SBT to address the device with on a computer routers, for example. And we already have an IP connectivity through Wi-Fi. And now the protocol that we're going to discuss about this communication from use Win32 to Cloud. What are the different protocols which are used? And I'm also going to give you most popularly used political names over here. I'm not covering the of communication in the context of discourse. So here we are talking about Wi-Fi connectivity between Yosemite to the cloud. So there are three very popular use protocols which are employee maturity. And it should be in terms more advanced message protocol, amputating arms, sort of message skewing element to support. And you know about the hypertext transfer protocol on hypertext transfer protocol secure that it should be as they should it be is usually be tied sent and received to get and post request. And this by far is the simplest of all the communication protocols. However, it should be has its own drawbacks. The package size or the size of the message to send and receive the response is a bit higher than what is written. And you didn't. And therefore it shouldn't be. And also this seems to be the slowest among all of them. Then group is a very specialist protocol used when the latency on very low latency is large, but the most general purpose protocol are the most commonly used. Protocol in almost follow this instance are the winner of lota protocols its end duty. So what we are going to do now is we're going to see how we can send data to issue TB. We will also try to see a platform that supports it should be data transfer, and then we are going to give a little treatment to what is included. And then we will try to understand a platform. I'll try to create a project with the platform which supports intuitive protocol and send the information to him to do it. So we are going to see how we can send information from your strategy to using it as well as using muted. So I have shown you some of the cloud platform names previously and out of that this one is one of the most interesting ones, which is called it's pink speak, not called now textbook supports but imputed as the next step.

Project 1 : Temperature and Humidity Logging in Cloud

But in the free account it only supports issue and that is enough for us to do a lot of different experimentation which we are going to see now. So it is it takes three primarily gives you three data storage for interviews, maximum eight different information like let's say if you are creating a system or if you are creating a project for home automation or industrial automation, then it means that you can send it since that informations to vehicles. You can send information every 15 seconds faster than that is not allowed in the free account. And there are lots of different online apps which can be developed for analytics with things. So I guess enough of the box and let's try to understand what is in speak. So let me open a browser and let me look at the platform to speak. Now, as I was saying, you think speak is suitable for lot projects. If you open the page you will also see the same thing. Speak for lot IT budgets. It doesn't say things speak for lot products. It's variety projects. Now what is the difference? You will understand that when we create one system. First of all, let's see how you can start using things. So all you need to do is first go to the sign in options, and then if you don't have an account, then simply click on the create one project and have to put your email, address, your location, first name and last. Lastly, after that, it will send you an email for verification. After clicking that email, you will be able to create a password onto speak. It's very simple and straightforward. So what I'm going to do is I'm simply going to log in to my account over here. So I have an account on the script, which I will be using. And my boss, which. And simply click on sign in. So when you create a new account on spec, this is how something will look like. Definitely you will be going through all these examples and everything, but that is something we can do later. For now, let's just try to understand the basics of the fundamentals of things. You will see channels over here. You will see apps, devices and support. And these are some of the steps. Now, when you create your first account on things to begin with, you want to create your first project is one of the subsidy to date. So the very first thing you need to do is take a new channel. Give it some me. So let's say lot projects one then we then I just started down here temperature and humidity and cremation of mantle. The name and description is completely optional. Whatever you want suitable you can put your Q as mentioned before. Thanks. Which allows up to eight seats in a free account in a single channel. So for now it isn't able to be for films. Let's call the first. Well that's then. Well. It is also optional.

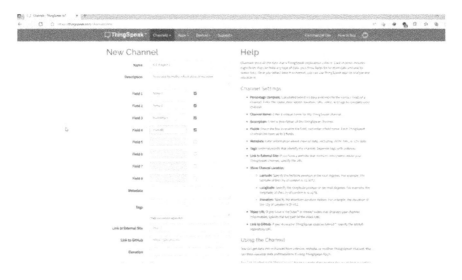

You can call it whatever you want them to. Then let's say humidity and humidity. Whatever you want, you can call it. Eventually, you will not be accessing this space by their name over here, but you will simply access them by three. One, three, two, four, three, three, four. Like that. No other changes are basically required. But you can, however, navigate as you may find. Which. Once this is done, it will save this channel. And as soon as you save the channel, you will see that your IAP dashboard has them created for you. Now this organized mode is coming up with, if you'll see, four different graphs of four different charts, so a available data monitoring system is ready for. All you need to do is start pushing information over here and you will see the data points right coming with you next time to see something. By sending information. Now, there are a lot, many other things. Also, if you see our visualization, then our widgets, we are going to see all of that later. For now, I will go to the API kids because first job that I want to do is I just want to see. I just want to send some value and see how it looks. And then we will see how we can do the same thing using SB 30. So see a light, a channel food if you go to a snack is you will find that ah, Hewlett-Packard's one is two right and one is still read and then there are sample API requests. So this is one for writing, this is one for reading and so on. What I'll do is I'll just copy this, right, channel food model and we'll try to evaluate this. Okay. I have copied it right click copy. And I will go to private. Now look me up on a notepad and just take a look at this link, what it's like. So if you see a step stupid, a production spec dot com question mark, then api underscore p is equal to some keywords and it done over here. Now let's look at the key again. This is the same API key that you have the right API over here. So you can use this one and simply replace the scheme with your account settings. And you can send some information and how the information is written. Look at this sample here and see the one is it. Let's say my first value. It's 11.5 degrees Celsius, my friend, when it's temperature. Let me put this directly. If I look up in this URL. And all you need to do is simply open a browser. Enter that all. I will go to private view again. You can see there is no data point over here. And I will simply hit enters. Now you will see the responses. One one. This foster quest has been sent. And now let's look at this shot in the sea. My first data point has been to distinct along with the date and time and as it. Now if you want to can send information on two things. Speak by simply moving like this and feel one. Can we add another one? Of course. Let's put it like this. And then two is equal to 25.3 if we modify the first one from 11.5 to 11.9. Let us add more face. And the three is equal to 74% and then the four is equal to 43%. Let's see all of it. Remember that this data will only be updated every so often. So let's hit this one. You get a response to just wait. You can see all four data points here. Now simply make some changes over here again. 11 points to 25.8 instead of 74. Let's make it 77 for serious looking for deflate again hit enter. Third request is gone and now you will see the data points again getting updated. Getting it. Now, if you keep using this request every now and then by making some changes, your first project is done. I know, I know you have not sent in ideal information, but just imagine if you can send your vehicle temperature information and with it information, then your data will start coming right over here. This is the bare bones lot project without sensors, without any hardware, which you can experiment to it.

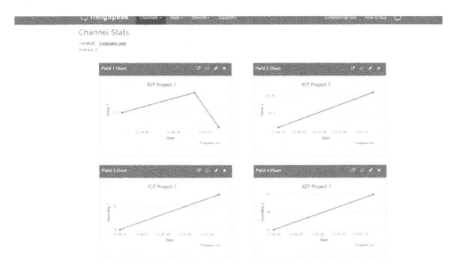

Now, of course, we will try to send this information through ISP 32 and we will try whatever is available in things speak to make our IOT projects more just.

SENDING VALUES TO THINGSPEAK FROM ESP32

We have seen the basics of things. We have seen the account creation on things. We are going to be held accountable to attract the cent. Some dummy panels, write a lot of things, pick a bunch, and this project will try to create up to them with sense the temperature and humidity information that we are getting from the HD one one or two to do sensor on button speak. Now in order to complete this program, you don't need any particular lab. All you need is the on one level of the issue to connect body and that's all. So this is the only library that you're going to need the boosters and stuff like that by now. Let's look at the code. Now, what I'll do is I'll also show you something which you should not be using. Okay. So let me show you. So there is also an official speak library which is provided for our DINO and I have distributed guides. Believe me, it's not worth it. So it will work sometimes, then sometimes it will be broken.

And if you're trying to use a program which shows this particular library, I would say, please avoid that program. The best way is to directly use the model for posting the town booking suite.

And that works without any favor. So just be sure that you don't get indulged into the celebrity Alderson Official Library. I'm telling you to stay on the assignment. Now, this is my. This is my dashboard. So if you know that I had created four different fields. But currently, I'm going to send only two values over here. So one will be temperature and another will be humidity. Now, let's look at the cool. We'll walk through the quarter completely. So this is the program that we're going to use. Now, if you look at the first two, three libraries, so this one is still active. I think if I going to find out about this one, it's to include the utility client library, which is helpful for us to post, which should be request. And this is the most elaborate. This is the DHT connection bin, which you know about, and this is the type of dish dispenser that we are using. Lastly, we create an instance of this level three quality HD so that we can use it.

```
File Edit Sketch Tools Help

sketch_mmpmmm_jmmmy

#define DHTTYPE DHT22   // DHT 22  (AM2301, AM232)

DHT dht(DHTPIN, DHTTYPE);

// Set your wifi name and password

const char* ssid = "Robotics Lab";   // your network SSID (name)
const char* password = "Robotics992";   // your network password

// Your thingspeak channel url with api key query
String serverName = "https://api.thingspeak.com/update?api_key=XXXXJOGUGHSYCYYU";

// Arduino some variables to allow us read and send data every minute
unsigned long lastTime = 0;
unsigned long timerDelay = 60000;

void setup()
{
  Serial.begin(9600); // Opens up the serial port with a baudrate of 9600 bits per second

  WiFi.begin(ssid, password); // Attempt to connect to wifi with our password
  Serial.println("Connecting"); // Print our status to the serial monitor
  // Wait for wifi to connect
  while (WiFi.status() != WL_CONNECTED)
  {
    delay(500);
    Serial.print(".");
  }
  Serial.println("");
```

Then you will see we have the A society or the I.D. and password over here. And this right over here is your thing. Speak. You want it. This is the entire one which we hitting before also. If you remember, the only thing that you need to add here, here, right over here is please replace it with your right API key. So you need to replace this last part with the key that you see in your account. Where do we see that? In API keys.Over here.So this one is mine. That's why I'm showing you this one. Apart from that, let remove anything unnecessary that I had. Right now I'm just going see, they'll begin so that I can put in some debugging messages over here. Then we are doing if I begin, this is the passage and then we'll print something that we are trying to correct as soon as and now the program or this part. It's basically as long as we not connected to why fine. Or what we do is my photo status will simply try to do my status. And if it is not connected, then we wait for 500 millisecond and some people in the dark on them. So that just gives a feeling that the product, as long as or the moment it gives connected, will get this message connected to. I find it to work with the IP address and what I do is I will also add a deliverable. So it will connect to your local pipeline network and then it will print the idea which has been assigned to the ISP today. Then what we do is we do the BSD dot begin function called which will initialize our use to 2%, which has been connected. Now I told you that free account of things will only allow you to send data every 15 seconds. So for every 15 seconds of data sending, what you need to do is you need to be it up 15 seconds after every iteration. So in my look, what I have done is if the line five status is connected, then we are going to proceed. How we proceed in what we post is mentioned over here. So it should be client? It should be. This is an instance of a library that we are creating. Then with the humidity and temperature, hence we bring them on to the terminal just to get an information about it. And now we create a you what of this is the scene you are told that you are going to create, which should be in the browser. So this data server name right over here then. And if anyone is able to add your first variable and includes golden and second variable, if you have and the tree and food four, simply go on and engage the same question. And then what we do is we don't bring in you are a lot C SGA. So the C is still basically passes the pointer to the string to this function. And now this will be you. And what will do it will try to get after this function. So here the big image. And here we try to hit the request after the request. Is it? We're trying to read that response into a sticky response. And this response score must be 200. So anything greater than zero, if the response scored is greater than zero, means we have some issue request, then we print. That is typically response code. If it is not greater than zero, then what we have to look into to look you. Then it should be the end and a delay of 15,000 millisecond or 15 seconds. So this will happen if it's connected. Otherwise you will get the message. I disconnected after every moment for a disconnected message. Let's look at the emails deposited milliseconds so that there is a difference.

```
?0 BUU
  WiFi_Thingspeak_DHT11

#define DHTTYPE DHT22   // DHT 22  (AM2302), AM2321

DHT dht(DHTPIN, DHTTYPE);

// Set our wifi name and password

const char* ssid = "Robotics lab";   // your network SSID (name)
const char* password = "xxxxxxxxx";  // your network password

// Your thingspeak channel url with api_key query
String serverName = "https://api.thingspeak.com/update?api_key=XXXXXXXXXXXXXX";

// Assign some variables to allow us read and send data every minute
unsigned long lastTime = 0;
unsigned long timerDelay = 60000;

void setup()
{
  Serial.begin(9600); // Opens up the serial port with a baudrate of 9600 bits per second

  WiFi.begin(ssid, password); // Attempt to connect to wifi with our password
  Serial.println("Connecting"); // Print out status in the serial monitor
  // Wait for wifi to connect
  while(WiFi.status() != WL_CONNECTED)
  {
    delay(500);
    Serial.print(".");
  }
  Serial.println("");
```

Otherwise, if the Viper gets disconnected in between, you will be hit with three or four messages. Now I have started uploading the code. It will take some time. Meanwhile, let's go to channel settings. And do you have the channel so that there is not a single data point on our channel? In our view. So this is my channel. This is the idea. Now the program is being compiled and then it will be uploaded to the to board. Now, this is the simplest and the most practical way to use things like that. So I would recommend using this way only. Once the program is uploaded with just open the city to monitor. Trying to see the outcome. Code is downloaded. Connected to our site with IP address. It's with temperature within humidity and the response score is to drench political support admins success. Now let's open this board over here and see if we can get the data point. So we have. Okay. The first one which we have sent this temperature on the second one, which we have seen humidity that's of stick and creating the channel. Let's call the first one adds temperature and the second one ends with it. After 15 seconds, you start getting another data point as well. So I don't think 15 seconds have elapsed.

So after 15 seconds, you will again see this message and that is this, humanity is this. And then this line and another response which. Let's see. And I given 15 I have given one additional. So that is 1 to 2 seconds. Let's remove that one and we applaud. Meanwhile, this is your things, big dashboard or what I can say is this is the first IAP project. So by default the name of your channel will come here. I project when I deposit and here is the temperature. You can also modify whatever you want to show over here. So the title is Let's roll them then I want to show. This is my room humidity. I did some tea, but I want to show. Let me see the quote. It's uploaded. It's going on. And supporters applauded. Now it is connected because the other data point, the data point it sends is also this 200 different data point right over here. There. You can see we have got the two points. This one is temperature and humidity by default. The charts over here will be automatically adjusted of dynamically adjusted. Just go here and play around with the settings, whatever you want to happen over here. So you can change time scale. You can change your average median. What do you want to display on X? What you want to display on y. So y for example, for us in Spain exits M in BGC. So in that way.So why it's. Value products and exits include. So this way you'll start getting the points. Now I am not even going into my Arduino, Paul, but as you can see, the temperature logging had started. Now, this is the Batman PIN Stick project that you will be doing. Apart from that. Of course, there are other things that can also be done, like you can add against weight. You can download the data into your computer and like many other things, we'll see that in the next project. So that's it for this project, guys.

What I'll do is I'll keep the same core running in my institute you do. And then we'll experiment further on this part over here. Till then, what I'm going to do is I'm going to keep this alive. It is coming so that I want to monitor the data for some time.

DATA VISUALIZATIONS IN THINGSPEAK

Now that we have seen a sample data uploading from things speak on from the as we told you to go things we cloud let's see what other things we can do in seed or apart from just viewing individual assertions. However, let's give this one thing in your mind. Whatever my experiences out of the kind of projects that I have gone to monitoring is perhaps the most important application people use a UTI for. There is a cloud control facility available, of course, but usually in industrial sense it does not use. So things speak of something which would turn out to be very good for you if you are creating an industrial project.

Now this is my dashboard, so I am not having the other at the end, so let me just delete them. So this is how I'm getting my data right over here. First of all, let's see what, apart from these two views we can have. So we can see there is an active visualizations button right over here and it should click that. You can see there are a number of different things which can be shown, as I told you. Now, if you don't go there and if you just go here on this tab, so there are visualizations and then there are widgets. There are some widgets which are built inside itself. For example, if I see a numeric display. And connected to frequent and let's call it room temperature. Then you will also be able to see a room temperature widget coming right over here. So it has been doing some rounding off. But let's take the decimal point temperature. And now it will show you an exact room temperature. In case. If you don't want this, you can also have a gauge. Previously we had to write down a good gauge code, but now it has got integrated in the thin speaker itself. So you can show the main value, you can show the max value of let's see if it is room temperature showed that the max value will never be more than 50, 55 or 60. You can also show something like that from range 35 and onwards of 35 to 68, which means it's 14, something like that. And then let's choose the unit as degrees Celsius and create a gauge. Now I'll just delete this one. So here we have a gauge against for temperature. And similarly, I can also have a gauge for humidity. So humidity is going to the genetics percentage. Lipsitch. Can you see that? This way you can customise your visualisation in a bit more fashionable ways so that you get to see some different visualization, some different look at the visualization. And if you want to go beyond that, if you really want to go beyond that, you can also go to apps and then you can go to visualizations and create your own visualization.

I don't want to go into that immediately now because I'm considering this to be a beginning of a new project. And for most of the industrial applications, if you have noticed how many visualizations is usually everything that is required and about from having visualizations. Another thing we want is to be able to export the data. Now you see you have this filled one fill to fill people for the time that you can export. Let me export the temperature data at CAC over here. And let's see how it looks like. Can you do some analytics about it? Can you do some operations about it? You definitely can do about it and just see. So this is the I.D. and this is a free one. You could all the pilots stored over here. Into this excel or see us.

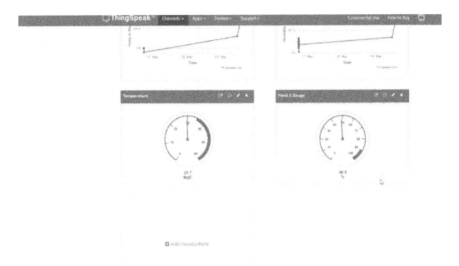

We find based upon that we can become more analytics, create more charts and visualizations in Excel or in any other way as you want.

WHAT IS MQTT PROTOCOL

Let's try to understand one of the most widely used protocols in IATA, which is called US MQ duty. Now, it is one of the standard protocols which is used by a number of different services, including of. Then Ahab Lewis And then almost all of the platforms do make use of nudity. Let's see why it is so significant. What's so beautiful about impunity so that it becomes so popular for using an iota. Now in order to understand MQ duty, first we have to understand the regular computer networking connection. And that's how a regular computer networking connection.

So there can be or there is an entity which we usually call S server and then there is an entity. It's usually called us plant. In a typical client and server application, then we have to exchange information. What happens is this client using some protocol which can be as simple as b c p socket. Are something like it's too deep. Can send some data over to. So what someone has to do here is import. It has to create some temporary or permanent storage of that bit. So server has to be a program. A complex program running over here in case of a strip.And a similar program in case of dispute. And that program will store the incoming data coming over here. Then if there is some other client, let me call it that's client two wants access to that same data. What this line does is then it creates a request to the server. And to which request the server will look for the data from the storage and. Reply back. Now, that's how a very simple and usual competent computer network will work at a glance. Configuration will work depending upon the protocol. The speed of glance over communication can be faster or slower. For example, a direct kinship connection or socket is very faster as compared to a CTP. But still the data has to go through all this processes. Now imagine a scenario. Then you want to have a single server and let's say there are one, two, three, four. Then. Or even 1000 different clients. All of them want access to the data coming from one another and creating a complex mesh network over here. So they may want data. So this tells them to need to move on data coming from this one. This excellent in terms of one data coming from one to me, one data coming from Poulsen and so on, it can be a very complicated in nature and therefore whenever such an application are demanding such kind of networking. In that case, what we do is we use something called let's impurity. Now how things work in impurity. Let's see again, if you compare it with traditional sense, there is not much difference. But let's see what we call the things here. So there is a server over here. Which in case of impurity, recalls.Broken. And then instead of calling these entities as clients for now, we will just call them as blank itself. So let's assume that there are two clients for now. What these clients do. It's instead of sending data directly to the server, then server breaking down that data and storing into some kind of database. The communication happens over something which is called topics. For example, let's consider our cars where we are rating temperature and humidity values. In that case, the topics could be. Temp and. Humidity. So if client one it's exacerbated by over here in my case, then what will happen? The sensors will be connected to the client. One. And it will trade the sense of value, then what it will do, it's it will publish over the topics called temp and humidity. So whenever it has to send the data, it will be called as publisher. So they never plant one sensitive data. It's called as a publisher, and it will publish using a topic called Temp and a topic called Humanity. So it will publish the temperature and humidity values. But whenever some other client now for example, this client two and let's say there is a client three. If they want access to this data, then they have to be subscribed to the topic that they want. For example, client three may want only humidity. Client two maybe a mobile application and it wants both temperature as well as humidity. So now this act or this two clients will act something, adds subscriber. And they will even subscribe to this one will be subscribe to both temp and humidity. And this slant over here will be subscribed only to humanity. Now see how communication happens. So whenever the planet one sends the data over to the screwed up stamp and humidity, there is no need to create a virtual storage over here whatsoever. Will do immediately or what this particular entity will immediately do. It's it will allow that incoming data over to all the subscribers who have subscribed to them. For example, if there is a temperature value called 30 and humidity value called 40, which has been published by this client whomsoever had subscribed to temperature and humidity, both the value will be instantly send back to them. So this land to at the same moment the publisher publishes it will read those two values over the fields. And this one will get only the humidity value.

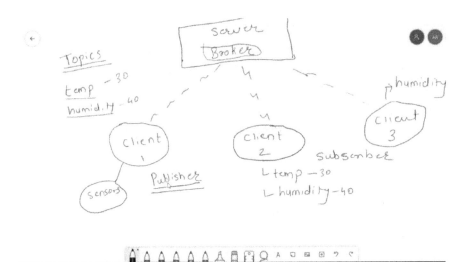

Without doing any kind of storage. Now such storage is optional, but you can definitely create a storage if you want, but it is not needed. And therefore what we call here, it's broken because it is not actually serving the data, it is just brokering the data, it is just exchanging the data that is coming from here to all those who have published all those that subscribe to it. Now, the biggest benefit over here is there can be as many topics as you want. And most importantly, a client can be both publisher as well as it can be a subscriber. So if it's sending the temperature and humidity values, but it can be published to a field called let's see and clients do. It's publishing the value of entry. So it is publishing the value to a lady like on or off, for example. And this client one had subscribed to the lady whenever on the mobile app I do the in on or off the send messages is given to broker. The broker will wrote it down to client one and depending upon that I can take my action that I want to turn the lady on or off. So the important point to remember over here is a client or any device. Can act. As publisher. As the LEDs subscriber. And since there is no storage involved and the major job is done as a broker, the overall spirit of communication in computing between sending the data from one device and the second device. Receiving it is very, very fast. This is Calder's message. Q Elementary transport. I'm not way into the technical details of the protocol. There are plenty of documentation available on the Internet to study about the technical details about it. I'm here to make things understand to you in a simple, conceptual way that's possible. In the next project, what we'll do is we'll try to create an application using it so that the things are much more easily understood to you if you want to go into the detailed documentation. I will also provide the required documentation if you want, just email me about it and I'll send you the official home duty technical protocol duties. But that's not needed for most of the developers. So all you need to do is read to understand exactly how it is working and you can create an app for it.

ADAFRUIT IOT PROJECT - PART 2

Now that we have created an entire dashboard for our usage, now it's time to send some values to this dashboard using honor code. Now what? I'm going to do it before you do that. Before you do send those values to here, let me just go to profile ones, because you're going to need or instead of going profile, you have to go to this project over here, which is called Mickey. Now when you go to myki, it will show you your username. Mine is on me. Try not to do it. And then the reason you keep this key is basically your authentication to the amputee broken off. That's what you have to use this.

You have to copy and paste it in your code. Now I will switch to code, will try to understand the code first and then we'll try to see the. Now, this is the code over here which we use for our purpose. First thing I will do is I will walk you through the inside and before I walk you through the entire. Then we also show you the required circuit that you need to hit on this particular expert. Look at it. So we have everything. Just like before DST. It's connected to GPO 27 and this really is connected to the number.

Circuit Wiring : DHT22 and Relay

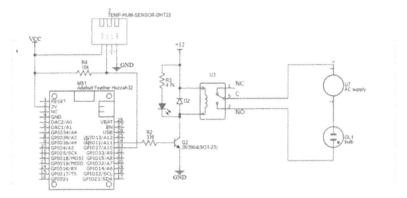

So through this 27 number which read the temperature and humidity values and to this number 12, we will be able to control the release if needed. You can definitely go out for adding more sensors and more release as we watch. Now this particular quarter will require a utility. You most probably will already have that included celebrity as a part of our diet. If you don't have that, simply go to include library managed libraries and here you will have to search for ADA through Underscore and Q-Tip. This are a level that is given very enough, but they are not restricted to be used to it in a food server and you can use them for other purposes. The fruit and beauty. And you just have to install it. I have 1.3.0 installed. If you face any discrepancies, then try to use 1.03.0 and let me know how it works for you. Now the first two lines are basically my flying fuel into the ditch and in good the decline dotage with all the good lines. Then this is the wife credentials. These are big enough for all your credentials.

```
#include <WiFi.h>
#include "Adafruit_MQTT.h"
#include "Adafruit_MQTT_Client.h"

#define WLAN_SSID      "Abcdefgh xxx"   // Replace it with your WiFi SSID
#define WLAN_PASS      "hhhhh.xxxxx"    // Replace it with your wifi password

#define AIO_SERVER      "io.adafruit.com"
#define AIO_SERVERPORT  1883                   // use 8883 for SSL
#define AIO_USERNAME    "smitrana3140"  // Change this to your username
#define AIO_KEY         "aes5492c74e5450c3f0ab7ee2a30958550133"  // Change this to your key

#include "DHT.h"

#define DHTPIN 27 // dht connection

#define DHTTYPE DHT22   // DHT 22  connected to pin 27

DHT dht(DHTPIN, DHTTYPE);
int rel = 13;
```

So you will not change the name of service. You will not change the board of server. You will definitely change the username and the e-mail. This key should be the one which I just showed you over to you. So this activity must be copied. And listening to your call like the look you. Once you do that, the inevitable later things are over. Next is you see the regular one. You draw the standard edge. Then the DHT bin is 27. The sensor type is 22 and recreate the instance of DST sensing. Lastly, we have an ADL which is to connect. And I'll just remove some comments to not make it difficult for you.

```
#define AIO_SERVER      "io.adafruit.com"
#define AIO_SERVERPORT  1883                   // use 8883 for SSL
#define AIO_USERNAME    "smitrana3140"  // Change this to your username
#define AIO_KEY         "aes5492c74e5450c3f0ab7ee2a30958550133"  // Change this to your key

#include "DHT.h"
#define DHTPIN 27 // dht connection
#define DHTTYPE DHT22   // DHT 22  connected to pin 27
DHT dht(DHTPIN, DHTTYPE);

int rel = 13;

WiFiClient client;
// Setup the MQTT client class by passing in the WiFi client and MQTT server and login details.
Adafruit_MQTT_Client mqtt(&client, AIO_SERVER, AIO_SERVERPORT, AIO_USERNAME, AIO_KEY);

// Setup a feed called 'photocell' for publishing.
// Notice MQTT paths for AIO follow the form: <username>/feeds/<feedname>
Adafruit_MQTT_Publish temperature = Adafruit_MQTT_Publish(&mqtt, AIO_USERNAME "/feeds/temperature");
Adafruit_MQTT_Publish humidity = Adafruit_MQTT_Publish(&mqtt, AIO_USERNAME "/feeds/humidity");
// Setup a feed called 'onoff' for subscribing to changes.
Adafruit_MQTT_Subscribe relay = Adafruit_MQTT_Subscribe(&mqtt, AIO_USERNAME "/feeds/relay");
```

Here, you create a modified plan and then you create an absolute amputated land to this land. What you have to do is you have to pass on your plan. This is like the sort of across the board number username and so that's passage. So all those values are already mentioned here we are just passing it right with you and also passing it like, okay. And then what we do here is we set up of this over here. So my first route is temperature, second visibility, third is remember the name temperature here is actually not important. This is important. The address of your feet. Now, how do you know it is forward slash grooves, forward slash temperature. Let me just go through my feet. Enough, you. Just hover over this thing and just notice this corner over here. So humidity when you see down the bottom left corner of the screen. Let's see. It should be, as I noted, as a dot com slash slash schools slash humidity. You can have as many food such as you want. You may have multiple layers, which I don't currently address of this food. If you'll see here, it's slash roots, slash humidity. Then what is my lamb? Slash foods slash really day and room temperature for slash foods for slash temperature just to mention them as forward slash routes temperature or slash severity for slash foods. So if you have more of them, simply create more such instances. Okay. Now let's go to the court. So the urgency, the terminal beginning. Then we created a relay output when initialized as our footprint made it low. Then what we do here is we again do the same thing we had done before. The one photon beginning was the Sabian password here. We wait here till we connect to I-5. Once you connect to I-5, we simply show them.

Or we simply print the Fentress over here. Once that is done, what we do is we subscribe to a particular topic. I hope the concept is clear to you. So here we want to subscribe to the topic really and we want to publish to the topic temperature. I mean, so here we have subscribed to the topics and then we do the student figured. This is an important. Now this amputee connect is a function which you have to keep calling your void min also low protein so that whenever the loop executes it will check its impurity. Connection is alive. Not if it is not alive then you will have to reconnect. So therefore this is composite. It must be there on the. Now here we have created a subscription. This function is very interesting. So you create the subscription and you just wait here until some time elapses and then you check if you have received some data or not. Now, mind, well, mind. It's currently only for really just checking one subscription. If you have more subscriptions, you'll simply copy, paste this and that if look again. So I'm checking if the subscription had some message. Yes, we do have. Then we print on the serial terminal what we have. So we may not last through. Will give me the value of the feed. I have written some code here that if string compare that will last it is on. Then I will turn on the relay and with the message I'll see that if the extension computer string comparison of the relay not lost luster the value it's off. Then return of the end will simply print on the terminal literally has been done. If you have multiple ones, simply repeat this if loop next time your subscription would be sitting in reality, things like that.

```
// Ensure the connection to the MQTT server is alive (this will make the first
// connection and automatically reconnect when disconnected).  See the MQTT_connect
// function definition further below.
MQTT_connect();

// this is our 'wait for incoming subscription packets' busy sub loop
// try to spend your time here

Adafruit_MQTT_Subscribe *subscription;
while ((subscription = mqtt.readSubscription(5000)))
{
  if (subscription == &relay)
  {
    Serial.print(F("Got: "));
    Serial.println((char *)relay.lastread);
    if (strcmp((char *)relay.lastread, "ON") == 0)
    {
      digitalWrite(rel, HIGH);
      Serial.println("Relay Turned On");
    }
    if (strcmp((char *)relay.lastread, "OFF") == 0)
    {
      digitalWrite(rel, LOW);
      Serial.println("Relay Turned Off");
    }
  }
}

// Now we can publish stuff!
float h = dht.readHumidity();
```

So this is my subscription park and ziggurat here. And then here it is. I'm reading the humidity, I'm reading the temperature. And then simply, if not temperature not published, it wins what I'm bussing or I'm calling the function temperature not published. This is the food name and this is the function and passing behind you at speed here. If it does a nonzero value, then it simply means it has been page. So it's not temperature of less than ten, in other words. It is okay. Similarly, my second value humanity seem to if altruism has been exuded here. If you have some of the values which you have of losing, you have to defeat these two evils. Things. Here. I publish the impression he never missed humidity. And then I'm printing some asterisks, and I'm taking a delay of 5 seconds. And after the IOC ends, we have 2 seconds of the middle console. One. Thank you for time. Let's make it three. And lastly, this is the amputee connect function. Don't make any changes to it. It will simply check if it is connected. If it is connected, it will simply return. If it is not connected, it will try to connect to the. And the code is pretty strict, simple and straightforward. All I am going to do now is I'm going to upload this into the board. I will see the output.

ADAFRUIT IOT PROJECT - PART 3

Now my quote uploading is in process. I have just done the camera turning on and you can see let me just set it once. Okay. So connecting to robotics lab. This is my heart. A bit connected. I got an IP address. Then it is not yet connected. So it is a train duty and also connected. Let's just go through here. This will see some values over here coming. So humidity, it's 50.60 and temperature is 29.90. And the same values we should be able to observe over here. However, we are not. So temperature is correct. You would. It is not correct. Let's see. What is the problem with humidity? I'll go to Dashboard.

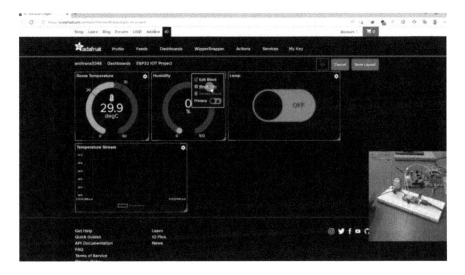

Let's just do the shoot again. So what is the problem with this roadblock? It's connected to humidity, food. Next step.0 to 100. All looks good here. So foods you read Dee dee, deedee. Keep in mind if everything is good with this filename so we can see temperature but we can not see humidity. Okay. I can understand the reason. The reason is very simple. We have published them back. Me? You shouldn't be doing that. So let me just put a delay here of 3 seconds.

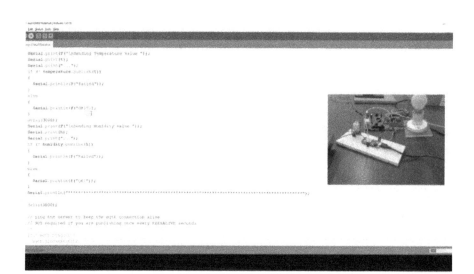

So it is basically throttling the the free account is throttling because I'm trying to send two values back to back. So if I did deliver beer, I should reduce this. But just let's keep it as it doesn't matter. So we have sent temperature and then we are waiting and then we will send humidity. Now let's wait for the record to be uploaded. So connecting uploading is in progress. Once the uploading is done, the serial terminal will become active. We get to see some status connecting to the working slab connected connecting to MQ duty failed retrying and due to connection in both the connected. Now it will send temperature first and then it will appear 29.90%. Then humidity 50.00 is also okay. Now, let's refresh this one over here.

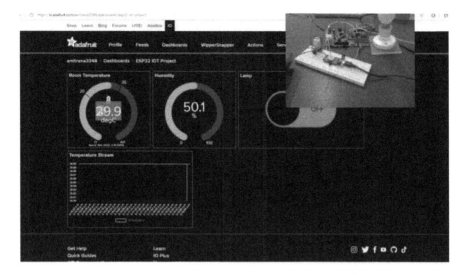

Now, as you can see, we have both the pilots. You have temperature here and we have the humidity over here as well. Now, let us also try this switch. So the switch is basically supposed to push back some values. So I'll just keep this one over here. Let's skip all three windows here. So there is switch. It is still terminal. And here is the. All. So I'll just turn this lamp to on position.

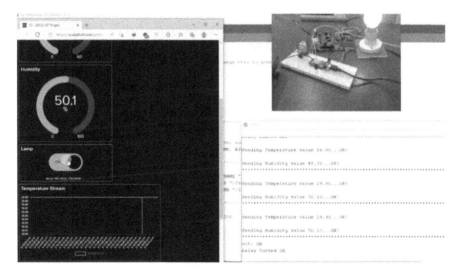

You can see. Got on. Really turn on. Can you see how instantaneous that was? It was a few of the billions we have in our program.

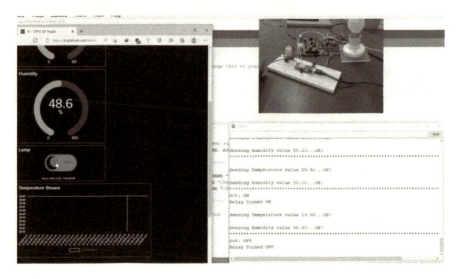

See that. So fast. Now, this is just one thing. Okay. If you see, I don't have or I have not utilized this on board illegally over here, and I can do that as well. If you have to do a list of changes, what you will do, it's in. So let's let me take LSD and let's call it a lady and the school building. Okay. I'll just use a little bit in the name itself. So SEPTA.Been more.And underscored belief in Goma output. And let's do digital right entity. And those were built in Goma. Look, I'm very doubtful whether this is too high or too low, but let's do it this way. So now that we have it in there, we will also have another feed. Emily let's call it anything like that. Okay. Changes in the code you have subscribe to relay here. So you will subscribe to entity here. And here we will just repeat this. So I told you, the reason I'm showing this to you is because if you want to make changes and if you get stuck somewhere, then this should help.

```
// Ensure the connection to the MQTT server is alive (this will make the first
// connection and automatically reconnect when disconnected).  See the MQTT_connect
// function definition further below.
MQTT_connect();

// this is our 'wait for incoming subscription packets' busy subloop
// try to spend your time here

Adafruit_MQTT_Subscribe *subscription;
while ((subscription = mqtt.readSubscription(5000)))
{
   {
   if (subscription == &relay)
   {
      Serial.print(F("Got: "));
      Serial.println((char *)relay.lastread);
      if(strcmp((char *)relay.lastread, "ON") == 0)
      {
         digitalWrite(rel,HIGH);
         Serial.println("Relay Turned ON");
      }
      if(strcmp((char *)relay.lastread, "OFF") == 0)
      {
         digitalWrite(rel,LOW);
         Serial.println("Relay Turned Off");
      }
   }
}

// Now we can publish stuff!
```

So subscription and really. And they did not lasted. And they did not last through here in this building. Then it lasted, and then here and under school, built in. So we have everything written as a change to the code for LSD and stuff related on it should be turned on and turned off and everything is done over here. I will also reduce this genius furthermore to let's say, 1500. So that will see further, faster court execution. And while this court has been applauded, what we will have to do is, you know, we will have to go here. And we will have to create a new block and connect to a field on a new field called Ellie. Let's take a toggle switch and let's create a new feed called entity. We can create the feed directly over here. So let's call it relative unknown. Then the button has been created, inserted below. Let's stick it over here. Let's review some sites so that they look a bit business. And save the lunch. Now let's check whether we have the code uploaded. Yes, it is uploaded. And immaturity is also connected. And potential value is coming your way. Then it's come. Let's start again. Lam turning on your city. It's. And is the happening on? Okay. We'll have to close the lamb to check then, but I guess you have seen it. So if you sugarcoat the reality, it's no fun. Any return off. And the return on.Lantern on, lantern off. So that it's, my friends, a complete lot project that you can build with the research you do and some simple components. Now again, there are a number of different things that you can do in IO, but we'll see that in our next.

ADAFRUIT IOT PROJECT - PART 4

Hi. Now that we have seen a complete project over here with idea, let's go a bit more in deep two. Okay. So you have seen that you can have a line chart, but a gauge and no values like that. You can have multiple different. Balance multiple different charts over here. So you can also have a stream of data coming here, line chart coming here and things like that. Now, if I go, let's say to room temperature, particularly this one here, then I will be able to see the inset chart off temperature values right over here, if you can see.

So usually in an industrial or any real time, I will not find the data being sent so fast. Okay. We usually send once some minutes or not even months of my expectations for compliance so far have been sending data once, 5 minutes, 10 minutes or 15 minutes. That's usually fine. Now. Again, if you don't want to purchase it, I'll and if you have to share this to your client or with your customer, you can do that. How? Let's, for example, this is something you have created and you want to give your client access to this.

You want him or her to see this, but you don't want to give them any access to this controlling mechanism. But they should be able to look at the look and feel of this. What you can do in that case is just go to this. That's what it is, controls. You will see that it's not more load just to make your look and feel the way you want. But the important point here is Dashboard. So currently it is locked. If you unlock it, it will make all your friends public and you can simply share this link to a client and they can access it. Let's see a demo. So what I'll do is I'll just open any other browser. Locally, it's still better. So we have not logged in here, and I'll just press this link over here. And we will see. We can still see the dashboard. To see streaming data on designs you will need to create telecoms. I don't want to create an account, but I can see something over here that gives me an access to it. Okay. I can also click on let's see, temperature stream and I can see all the values over here. If you notice, you will not see or even not get any more details like downloading or anything. However, this is a good start. You can give this to anyone. Just stresses. It's definitely control. Actions will not be available. Moreover, if you go into your food, any particular food, just like things, you will get a facility to download your data. You can download it as JSON or add CAC. Most of the times your client will do this on their card if they want to do something about it.If they want to experiment, something about it. And as I said, the basic analytics is present over here as well. So if I go back to my dashboard, this is my change that leaves you the way you want. Now, let me go to the actions part. So let's review on what actions are available. There is no action currently and yet in three account. So we have limited actions available. There are two types of actions. One is the reactive action and another one is a scheduled action, serial action. It's something which you may like to do once a day or twice a day or something like that. Reactive action. It's something of an analytical action that. Let's see if. My favorite temperature.Is greater than. Let's see. 31, then.Action. So what's your message to. Somewhere or some food or send a message that you can create a webhook for any other application.

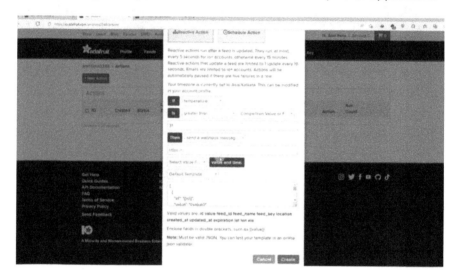

But in your broken. You can also see the email action. So just want to hear. Emily Currently this is a basic enough for my account, but a broken. If you create then you can also send emails to yourself from here. So pro account is not that expensive. Even with enough radio, it gets $10 per month and Alabama is a much, much affordable. What you can see back if you consider a customer, primarily an industrial customer for that matter. Okay. So this is about it. I hope you will experiment a lot with it. And I'm going to keep the synths running for my next experiment. So I want to use Alexa to simply control my lap.